Listening to the Stones

Nick Johnson
Bedeille (Sommet d'en bas)
8/8/02

Listening to the Stones

Her Gentle Slab

M. C.

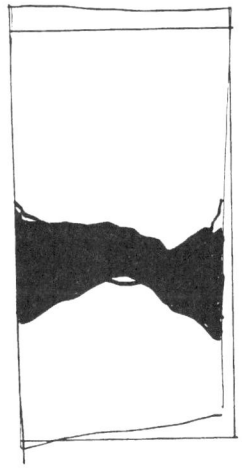

Nicholas Johnson

etruscan books

2010

First published by etruscan books

LISTENING TO THE STONES copyright © Nicholas Johnson, 2010

COPYRIGHT
No part of this publication may be reproduced without the prior permission of etruscan books.

etruscan books
Elm House
Stowe Lane
Exbourne
West Devonshire EX20 3RY
<atetruscan@aol.com>
www.e-truscan.co.uk

ISBN 978 190 1538 717

The publication of LISTENING TO THE STONES was made possible by a Writer's Award from the Arts Council, England

etruscan books are distributed by S.P.D., 1341 7th Street, Berkeley CA, 94710, USA, and are available from Collected Works, Level One, Nicholas Building, 37 Swanston Street, Melbourne 3000, Australia. <collectedworks@mailcity.com>

Cover by Kate Johnson
Frontispiece by David Stoker
Typeset by Robert W. Palmer at *Tuff Talk Press*, Bristol
<robert_w_palmer@lineone.net>
Printed at Aldgate Press, London E1

This compendium of earlier published works, excerpts from *Land* (Mammon Press, 1999), from *CLEAVE* (etruscan, 2002) and the full text for the first time of *Listening to the Stones* (Many Press, 1999). My thanks to Fred Beake for publishing *Land*, and John Welch who published *Listening to the Stones*, and to John Kinsella who encouraged me to go back to the manuscripts I'd retained of the book. *S.W.* was first published by David Berridge at Aloud, in 2006.

For the previously published poems in *Her Gentle Slab*, my thanks to Wendy Mulford and Peter Riley for editing *A Meeting for Douglas Oliver* (infernal methods, Street Editions, Poetical Histories 2002), Peter Begbie and Julian Warren for appointing me writer in residence at Arnolfini, Bristol, for *Starting at Zero, Black Mountain College 1935-1957*, *This is Real - Dream On!* an audio tour curated by Rebecca Marshall at Electric Palace, Hastings, and to Patricia Scanlon for *Uplift - a samizdat for Lee Harwood* (Artery Editions 2009).

Brian Catling and Sarah Simblett filmed the final performance of *The Lard Book* in 2002, and Rebecca E Marshall made *Haul Song : Family and Philip*, both featured on a DVD included in this book. My thanks also to Matias Serra Bradford, Paw Eg and Harriet Tarlo. From my time in New Caledonia in 1988, Helen and Marcel Brinon, and for recent kindness, Dave Norrish and Libby Fawbert. Many thanks for patient guidance to Kate Offard at the Arts Council and to my typographers R.W.Palmer and Robert Moore and printers Martin Grant and Martyn Young.

When morning came
he sent and brought me up
but the God stayed in the tent
where he was
on the shore of the sea.
the coast
is crowded
the month-long mouth
waves and works
at the beach, the bank.
everybody's busy by the summer
but
the high fire
and the coarse and grading day
closes the head
of each of all.

Bill Griffiths

1948 - 2007

HER GENTLE SLAB

in memory of Joseph Beales

Syd Barrett Refrigerator

*A velvet curtain of grey
marked the blanket where the sparrows play*

Syd Barrett

My wife does
push me
like a clematis
in a wheelbarrow
I see this in my wing mirror
as I pass the snivel salsa men
lots of them wicket-like
wicket-like as I look my nose
the scar where the rat
bit it where I slept
the scar where the rat
woke me to bloodbanners
on the bolster today

Camel tears
*I am not asking for the moon
or wrestling with the stooks*
go jauntily push me
I tell her pretty face
wheel me below the cobwebs
*you should brush them down
give young spiders work to do*

My wife has filled
the pram with lawn
I want a
bargain
Silver Tongue

A mean spirit
levelling the sauce
I crackt on my potatoes
whelp & tussle
my wily wife
acorns sensibility
& summer fruits

    Come travel unnecessarily
she kisses you
on both sides
of the head
you might like that
but cargo out
to the moon sphincter
...it's just the waste pipes you see
...as you...unravel

Hiccup and cup
little green fellow mouse
tie a tie to your cheer
oh no little braid
how many saucers of lucozade
do you feel dismayed
at the ruin in your pleats
elusive treats?
come out like the Mint Garden in shade
without the luminous feats
of venture
the voyage snubber on the bi cycle
taping the shellac of our recording
overlaying the voices and fine mesh
in front of the horse's face
to keep flies from his nosy soot

scare me overcast me
tie my spire to the spade blade
red soil red soil can't drink Schlœr
juicing off my cheek
off rain off earth off peak
come spread out your cups
lets have our sups

one more day one more day
is all I ask I reel in a dab
of lemonade sent to my ear
cough cough and Bring me down
I am elusive it is
a solemn oath

my wife does roll up her sleeves
to do a good job of top of the trees
and fly around the heavenly sprees
the children do make on one of her knees
oaths and tabulations jump on the wing
it is enough to make a spraint to sing
a splint to cup and look at my ear
Brandy boy there is the *domino*
of all our nice behaviour gone

= = = =

The tractor rolled
thru your sweet hair
as you lay in the sun
    beyond the chasm
and turned to the time
    when men did no damage to their heads
Today was listless
you were passing the hill
beyond the caterpillar tracks
of the works site
you painted for HERNEAU
& you would wrap your hand around a
handle
of kedgeree   today is tonight
and you have closed the door
on a strange and stately fire

phew
lips go round teapots' blemish
places nostrils do find

tippy
    golden
I-am-sad-and-shivering
in my chainéd mail
piteous neckerchief
tied round my kneelybone

= = = =

Paper sheets
    paper greets
on haughty sidesteps
I must
part these cloisters

to a handkerchief of icicles
left by the millpond
you quiver because this
ebb is
underlined

in an ornate of winter
your throat is a gadfly
thrust into winter's
sleeves
your throat neck turns

= = = =

The sun is stepping down
with razorbill in its loins
I look at your refreshed lips
and see how your mouth moves
but I can't kiss you,
can't even ask
...the sun is too bright for your eyes
...there are cottonwool flecks that drop
on the garden
without rain on the telephone
and you go because you choose to
your lips unkissed

canvas
below viperbabies
hanging swirl
off the gooseberrybush
in sunlight the caterpillar hood
won't cover the head
or protect
from gouts of canvas

    = = = =

Golden stair
way and   what is there
to lose
and listen to?
put your ear to the amplified soil
from there dandily go
down hushedly the golden
stair

past the steam of
crumpled cafés
foxgloves wither in drying soil
which is red
and now Ju / ly is dead
and the season is square
and love plucked off the rind
and dropped from your fe / male
fing / ertips
and now Ju / ly
it isn't worth
a fly

look at your lips
and the way you kiss
will always be
a veryspecialthing
to me
as your mouth is seperated
from your face   expressing
a glance
I wish to kiss
   This

small curve
under feather
both lips
absolute breath
twenty years
then never

go to the storm petrels floating sugar cubes
turned into water snakes
under the tread

between your toes
in the shall / ows
where the shade blackens
alongside water grass

play the tune ping the song
it shalln't be long
the resolute

= = = = = = = =

In the silver shed
sweat runs down
walls to my little hand
cup it and lick it
no one will see
sweat land on your knee
you pull out your flute in the sun

care ess
before you carve
look out the window some one comes
lean out the window jaded quite suppressed
Don't you see
WHEN YOU LEAN?
only
a labradoodle
cock and stretch
her leg

would you stick
some wine stained curtains
up   over the shed?
let windfalls plop
on to the roof?
snag on their tooth
THE CORE, THE CORE!
lean and look, vague into the heart
of the granulated
light
leaning on
the silver
window cill

Work Don't Worry

The boat and the prayer
the bairn and the slate
the easel and the poster paints
the mother and the kid

and the cart goes thru
the teeny lane
and a bone lies in
the doggy's mane

up the cart   its convex
shape   with a ladder
at either end
a straw pile and a dog
a wheel and a steerer
a helmswoman and a light –
that pricked the heart,
but later enlarged the sex
the womb he cupped and later still
it was a bath upon the hill
of tin with poster paint on the out
side it was in a breeze but they were nude
and the light was clear and clean

look at the confetti
pouring up from the plug
on a coloured stream
at a helm she guided
watch the course of the underpin
the towing to be done, her head
his shoulder   the woman and man
where do they live how do they know
when shall they part
why should they feel
adrift and a howl

II

Scrotty blooded girl
the cat steps with its tail-half aloft
and touched Lego a lot, in front of the
charcoal boxes, the Quare   ah but
sniff, about its sleek head
look at the pink nude sketches
the liable do pull
                and paste the
                        nude man

or are the sunlamps
two eyes
and
the reclining man just
a pair of lips?

little boat
under blue
Mast. Cross
into the
Border
Those dots that
Hang

The boards of the cart
The dog below
The wood
lift your legs
around his waist

over to thou
all slide and slip
into the waters thee
Tide and the dark

Abstraction du Temps

Un bout d'orient, abstraction du temps, de l'espace.
Non pas une quête individualiste de mieux être.
Juste une rencontre, une curiosité ...

S. E

  A skewer of light pierced the gold oval table beside your bed I
was woken by a school party on a June Sunday morning near Le
Goutte d'Or where I thumbed my nose at you and grinned in the mirror
as you sat while my hair got cut & smartened
  Who trod in broken glitter on hot pavements of your city
and sauntered through archways of Parc Monseaux, and said I don't
Want a poem to mock-at-me, mock-at-me,
I laughed as electric light tongued outdoor statues at the Louvre
who watched workers snatch sleep in shifts
       behind service vans : but who then surveyed
street people
heard their breathing rasp in saturation following a heatwave,
in their tents, I did, did I then?

  Patently I encountered your city, your series of kingdoms in a line
of photographs on your wall,
to the Magrheb hills you climbed
and when you meet her you must look at her walls to see if there's a pair
of prints, identical or a pair, for that is what the two red playing cards
did signify
  Ah ha breathe incumbent, breathe through the brush of your
teeth to stir in anticipation of the splay of your sheets
I listened in the cool of your room to Rachid Taha coax up music, rev up
groove patterns
and he did roll his tongue and Kuti trumpets surged to draw lugworms
from his phantasmal throat
  I looked on your grey blue eyes which did edge stealthily like
halts between a camera shutter
       and the precise cool Beat of your heart
those small curving hands, you beautiful one

    Which bare feet did sashay down from place Dalida and throughout place Abesses
over a fall of stairs that had rancid glazing sugar on its curve
vervain smelling capotes in a dilapidated café
and let it be stated that though my fallacy is all too obvious my libido is a sweep
for the unsoothed arrivant who had his heart go jolt
and who decided to approach with a presence that constituted grace
if he were to be received :

who did learn your door code by heart in seventeen seconds
who was due to meet you on Friday in rue de Douaï where Jean Vigo cut *L'Atalante* in 1931
at the blue door in the long street of guitars
who had begun to articulate the *essence* of your face, your olive skin
embossed with the scent of the city and your appetite

    Which way did I turn when I saw you leave and descend steps to métro Clichy? turned back to watch you, to accept that soon I would see you leave and you had turned back too,
and my eyes were full of my feast
that I had no exactitude of how it would be served but would that be kind, without piety?

    'You have got darker' she said, and we drank lager from petite cut glasses we talked with a violinist, in interval from playing a concert at Messian's Eglise Trinité,
POINT, PAS REGULAR walking rue Pigalle to sleep in magenta sheets
and listen to the distilled sound
barely discernible of your breathing

The Five Squibs

On being precise and not
barging into nailhooks

coughing sputum
to the aether.

A trail of honey suckle
leads to black clouds and no stars
I can't see if it is snowing.

       On being precise, sinuous, tactile and
having an extraordinary range
       of misconceptions
          Persecution complexes
putting fright to bed the frisée lettuce to bed
and spooking my horse
Old Archipelago
(the name of MY horse)

I get despondent when I see a pencil
come shaping in grey spores of Cumberland
Saffron Walden. Violet. Damage vein
   the cousins I sleep and grind with
Oxygen they give me : and resuscitation.

Pencils hack at my Folgate, paper and rupture margins
Shavings and lather.
Foam; pyres not beacons, brandished burning tyres.

Pencils come to me
with the sealing of elephantine flesh
hacked down to size to point the ivory of unhappiness
and hand breastplates to cautious sailors who really are on

a re enactment of a flop-out naval disaster
oh lord your botched labours

despair what quality it has
and now the elephant rolls a tyre through summer dust

Solde   Whole Sale

Wipe out the shutters
                let sky in
with its florins and its wasps

drowsy in the jets
of milk on wax floor boards

                Bind
my mouth with a rudiment

a colander on the jailered grass
spinach under the sprinkler

Nose up the price the precipitous and pre
cise Bourgeois Louise Cough Linctus
        YOUR MIGHTY SPARROW amaretto,
THE GRANULES!!
Enjoy your paraffin surface

The Ultimate Adrenaline Adventure

Herons on the field on a silver hedgerow.

What was ultimate
couldn't be decoded, at a crimson watercourse some turned their eyes from
or others quietly considered :
plenty remarked how bright it was.
'I have grown up. My life has filled out.
'Severance can't belittle me.'

                What was there to be belligerent about,
                if you could enjoy these types of adventure?

        To abolish the larks and tongues
the ice caps and the
tumours
  why did You
   feel you had a responsibility
'I am countless.' Count me in.
'I wish you could.' Roll me over on the
lino. The vinyl.   Then this gravel.
the heaven chutney
          tangy for my stethoscope pasta
          and half price Parma ham

        To abolish larks and
  sky motes   garden centres
   and pleasurable
        clay pigeon
           shoots

Scythes in gorse bushes, treacle a domain
   where a visor lets in the pale rain and outs a refrain
adjusts itself to where a stately swathe of viper-young
   outpour scales in flanks metamorphoses to a handkerchief
upon the face and others cling and lean to
   a set aside field and where the predators whirr
and masticate feign it is true in dynamic islet flow
   thru' chutes of pearly cut outs in a refractor strimmer
tidying the waste so spilt to an unnecessary
   chute where it is rolled between the fingers and the thumb
screw of marking time and skelping a prairie domain
   outlandish this is the caustic outpost calibre
deer embeveller emblemic disregard the outpiped
   pipistrelle flow behind the hand shielding the young
skinned face from the setting milksun all across
   the prerequisite pink opacity. The spoils. This is in the throat
the lemon pith sinking without the gin taken
   dutyfree on the ousp of the water's surface
the tall domineering volume of currents taking the
   boat which midwiches had let the moorings
subside on because they were no better than
   gypoes crested in hereditary betterments
a rindcut off the birch lofted above napes
   succinct and damnable with no clearer
haven defined in a double rollover
   assessment of the influx and disembarkment
of coin lavered on each tithe
   the fields plurally held in a precise
fortune capsized due to *Barings*
   a nitrate mouth that fell due to bad counsel.
He held his arms above his head to declare
   a *pax* it was a brash hearing
a regulated chancel and so many
   traitors could stand on one floating cube
a prison fortress coming
   to an assessment of how the saline qualities
mattered, if you didn't
   issue a pastoral holding somewhere
beyond the intefada or the vista

Pantone 6 2 7

Silently
I came in   through a door beyond linoleum
silently   I showed my face
The chicken bone woman, tall eyed
knocks a clout nail in a sign she's fashioned
        BABY, DO NOT DISTURB
                        mounted on a enamel door
to a nursery   occupied   mouth o-ing the sheet/
   metal thru metal   banging wakes the house
& some one with a dense head remembers,
phantasmal layers minûte air, chambers in the brain, we are all,
soaked, he said – 'S'like living in a sponge',
engenders locution tele scoping inwards to closure
but not disinclined to read pages of this Radon book

breathing early a
ham catarrh cold
sweating the tongue
dissolution of brain monasteries

Dark and flooded it has been up to you to bring this fleet home
using your hand as a paddle. The luxury of rowing
through stale air of quarters
habited by the grandparents.

'Oh I know Tavistock. Used to go there myself, often,
and graze about in antique shops.'   If only she did.

Take your pick of tuning your ears to radiator pipes or turtle doves. A dream
picks up a momentum. You need to keep going. At every twist in the road.

early earlie morning   Dowsing
standing still outside the enamel door
pressing hands together eyes wide shut, wrists flopping back
hair sparking on his nape and up right leg thru a
font electricity   (They placed a font in this corridor in
13   12 (& built a church in this corridor)
                and placed a bee in his mouth
   red strawberry   threw the baby's shoes on a compost heap
in a Sundial garden.

There is fresh meat in the conservatory. Saddam chops.

 flurrie of wings carbonate dovecotes
doveshit equals grey green of a mouse's kidneys
cherooted on the kitchen floor   black and white tiles are pressed down
'As servants before the war
 we sank from duty
 we sank from authority'

The wind is viol. Curling with its waters rocking böw
over Arlington Court, the Valley of Rocks (Lynton)
Dulverton
Bucks Mills Lee Bay

October 28, 2000 cropfields flushed away in storms
— maimed pencil lines of once prow(d) field architecture
'I found my son gassed in his car. He'd farmed too long,
good come
great smile
  Osprey feathers   white white
     a barn owl low down swoops

I look at white scabs of water
at Barnstaple
interspersed with kayaks full of gulls, chewing thru pea-gravel
to dig out discarded Rotary Club food. Today is a breeze block day
& smells of overdate bubble gum

KodaChrome
      cold birthplace. Listening to the chip-chip of skate boarders
Sun turns sand pink.
Estuary
a stained glass silo that is above derricks and foundries on Northam hill
spume flows in from Ashford and the waters of Norwalk virus
'we are afforded views because we keep moving'.

The Lighthouse and the Clam

Crows hang
from orange string,
mottled by the sieve
of decompose,
prince sun shines
thru
their awkward
talons

I click
my fingers
to a flax oil dog
ahead of the lane we go
our lives are raked by our nosodes

We sit eating haricots
he bought in from the garden at
lunchtime, our lunchtime, today, is
this a joke? he is no longer here

In a barn I saw her
hair swept like a beauteous
hearth she was full
of promise
we stalked
each other's limbs
and crept up over us
a draining nursery song

Under sun glissade
sullen moods
permeate grasses where
gooseberry bushes scratch
      Ah white owl
you are dynamic
across the rotovators' blue
to the hurtle chambers
flit across the marsh
with a suiting case

Something important has occurred.
Zgougou's grave. Mattieu
buried Zgougou the cat; it wasn't enough
– he had to be honoured

It is lonely here
without my particulars
when death pitches her tent
and slugs chew the pastry jettisoned
after the final festival.
Tramps count knots in the grain;
once they shared
a language that rose
in the flesh
shared thru songs and synonyms
of battles feats
passions and dotteries;
but silver
struck some down
riddled the matted lungs
of syph and t.b.

On a promontary
the hand is laid   on the brow
her hand pats
the spine
nothing jolts
today

In a tree on Noirmoutier
the tree above Zgougou's grave
a roseate shape
a canopy embedded
a pilot or a bird will know
something special did occur.

"From the sand take some affection with you to Boulevard Raspail
"I search for ages for plain coloured
carrier bags
soon they will be outlawed." "Oh my love
I did go to the lonely part of the train for I am bereft.
Yet I like my own company." Now that he is dead

how do you think, how do you behave,
which part of the bed do you sleep on? When you were gone I moved
to your side.' We ate the haricots he picked
at lunchtime so it must be a joke that he is dead.

Old drains antagonise the silence
I wash my feet, slowly care
fully I switch the bolsters

'Our bodies are sexual, at every age.
That's important. The clam and the
lighthouse; yes it's beautiful here,
the gulls and the golden light.

The sea takes the lives. Some
widows lived first as demi-widows
in their anticipation; their men at sea
their men at toil. Look. Buy bottled water,
buy sand jars; help the sea wives' foundation.

Bye Bye Blackbird : Slight Return

In memory of Douglas Oliver

Magenta flock. Thru the mind pipes
king fisher darts over pram wheels in Place Stalingrad.
Cloacal ærials, porous streets
his tears flushed with apis

refrains what refrains – a form of assertion, this augurs
well, take the ceiling down
I do not want to see its hallucinatory glitter
I want to see some sky

Morphine alms.

Windowless, except for the bathroom
a postage stamp view of sky. Inhalation of city threadworms
his tinfoil trees pared from Seven-Up cans
But all-
encompassing magenta
as in the face as the voices went echoing out
thru the city pores you heard their resonance lodge in masonry
Later, further ahead, on the river dividing the city

On a mute
train
of thought, emblems of conversations; a return many had hoped for
– he'd been unable to articulate
disabled by multiple supervisions. And a king fisher optically bumbling on

Silence assiduous. Tongues
in the airless room. "And we made our own air,
jawing, the lovers – and preening. And then we were gone. We were the first
since the room had been re let. Putting salt down, spilting the wine"

Going to the zenith, holding your throat
up to the light that circled round it
[when the] king fisher flew across the red lance
of metal, above Seine, you reverted, to
the Holding Ground, but now you had no face

it had passed through various permutations,
        the person whose fate expanded saw his expression
was first to go; he saw it as his liquid tread
sprung off pavements and did not speak what it meant
when he got back to his room below
L'église St Vincent de Paul, to roost, but all he could
do
was crawl and slump and say : "I knew nothing about this.
I was suprised at that."

The king fisher, the alloy tree and the old bleached world
a diagram and a dream
of an enfant and a street,
ectoplasm frothing like retired S.A.S.
opposite Terminus Nord

radiant silt from shoe heels
kerklacking up the boulevards to one room with a sticky floor
    the litter outside Monoprix
          I'll take it all on
I'm still bouyant   I'll refill
your glass
& eat with you at sunset
        humous and sweetmint
            semolina and œufs florentines
                crême caramel and Irn Bru

caution me to say
        I'm primed for the best
not the worst
and I'll   I'll bespeak the past I'll meet with you
when the rushes make a sound in the earliest field
"and preach a little to the plates/
in autumn I'll clean my heart"

The morning air was cool, fridge-like and boy was it good
to get shot of that room – months you passed
supine in your bedding. Fingernails roseate
on tips of white digits that only felt life :
something that would not have troubled you
– or had a head been kneaded before it bowed?

Liaïson

She walks down the staircase
in a white skirt
and water is coming out of her clothes
dropping on the curve of the stair
There are
passionate eyes between her cherrybone toes
and in her mind silence is stoppered
              and does accept the rise and fall
of her mood. The walk is hushed
            and it is a short walk
                  and then we are back to conversation
                  and we have moved our chairs to a different place

And in the beautiful silence
no heat is lost no cast is made
it just flows like a bad lyric
to where traffic evokes the cut of the corn
on the lightly bruised hills
  and if that last line goes down as one of my worse, so be it,
I'm enjoying myself
on the lightly bruised hills
where a French lunatic sings out like a corncrake
ah how dumb
and our four palms splay out flat
                and I would recognise this meeting, call it a liaïson as
happiness or just
the suggestion of such

She walks down the staircase
like a bundle of lillies
cascade
and I look at her and see her smile
remembering previous happiness

Accidental Sightings

I

Empty of writing
Devoid of inclination
A tactile armoury
Closed and marred up
I queried : "Are you at my ear?"
This twenty sixth
Autumn. Since. Then.
Why does it? Go?
The branks o the branks
That pinion one arm
Part of the mind
To sleet and out
Down in the mouth
At the aether. Dis
Orientated.
A drift.

II

My mother left me when I was young
She has gone and is buried o
I could'nt regard aught but red Rightiho
And it took me so near the windy o
To its pane and to its gaze
And my heart's rising with tears I know
I can't mouth out their flow
I can't gesture much but cheerio.

Tight in my corner
Left as you could go
Dull is my collar
Through walls succour does grow

III

Concertina. You would release it
Because it's shut
Time like the lamp
Is rowing out

The old man unbowed undim
Inished unburdened not ashamed
Would not consent
To a proportioning hand.
"Guido, I knew you dead," he spoke.
"As lime, hard. And quite as spent."
The dust in the church porch
When children were born.

IV

Winter has come. Blue
Beginning. The light
Comes early
The day glass blown
And I get drained of writing
Shorn to the bone
To be shored up here
Stoic as stone

And I am empty of writing
Devoid of sense
A tactile armoury
Not at my dispense.

No, I will not walk with you
Not carousing today,
buying sweets in shapes of lips.
Today a hound at my heels
Wanted to declare a friendship
Ousted from the hunt, to defect but
You got him back to kennels
Where it belonged.
Suzanne's boy he rode on my shoulders
He was cross eyed much like his father then.
He liked the hound and he beamed
he saw it different than you or I.

V

I take my own form
Of complaint, dosed up to
This diagnosis this deterioration
In the head I clasp
I try to snap clean off.

VI

'I want to show you what I've brought'
The young school kid outside the window
Where I am, leaning in bed this morning
Turning the line to a lilt
Turning the line to a song
I know what waits me
When I get back. From my stagging night.

The engines are pounding
The sea is murky
It is thick and potage
The coast is not clear
The mind, like sails, smarting.
Clear. Thick. Near.
Fear does become an exhibit
Of bringing you to the identical place alone
And if you look closely
You'll see my face and hands are red.
Sortie and you are prone
To getting seized at the world's prow
If the world went by
If the world went by. A
Drift and gone. Maimed to the heart
Ravaged in the sternum or the lungs

VII

It is cold over Brushford
Where Gillard put down his pipe
Of gas to his car, where he did lie
And drift out to sleep and sleep.
It is cold with my love at the door.

It is cold without her shoes on.
The wind sluices through trees at Saint Mary's.
It is cold within Brushford
It is sleeting across the banks
The smir is up at Poundsgate,
And I'll be leaving in a while

VIII

Today. In the blue mewling
                        Afternoon
Stogged river banks' colour of butter
And this Scotch tastes of TCP
Down at the methane garden
When the red figure
Could've
Been Seen. Sylvanus Roskilly
Salathiel Pavey. Apprehended. Viewed.
The red male you just considered.
Rowan and elderflower. They are red.
Rosehip and torturer. This is red. And savage.
Stationary.

IX

A celebration
For the boy the boy
Who was eight by then
The white and pink
Meringues and fruit
Saladed with clotted cream
And a stained glass lamp,
Hair gel, pear drops and computer watch
Where are they now?

X

Emptied of writing
A cold air cuts through
And of what there is
To be hollowed by;
See, I become hollow.

For five excoriating years
Could there never be
A peace to write, had he
Retained
That uninnocent spontaneous
Thought

The innocence and
Rationale the boy's face had
But emptied of imagin
Ation Silence too, of that as well.
What a cold air a feast has
A rabble at the window
It is a maelstrom
Becomes apparent
"The maelstrom becomes you. See."
To countenance this in the silence
You would lean towards

To the Spirit of Andrei Tarkovsky

for Louis Johnson

How long you have held your head
heavy as a chain your eyes open
pointlessly for there's nothing to see
even here, but snow or sleep.

No child crouching over a stream,
heavenly mirrors to a woman's blonde hair
the bitter scents on trains, ah at least
you've nothing to draw conclusions from.

The sound of the hedgerow in your ear :
the fields, unponderous after the thaw
are the film maker's kingdom –
you walk with crow's feet to reach the interior

Look over the pebbles with me.
Nothing else is eternal. But here
the emptied out dreams, the laundry
of those butterfly wings, decaying.

Cooking grease would hardly stop
the birth. It heaves out and
you haven't seen my joke. Death through,
I'm not eternal. Take off my scarf.

I'm looking at the angle of pebbles,
intricate families of grass : the snow
says that death will be fresh, you
helpless as in birth. There's time to face it.

Als the Sadwe in the Undermel

February Monday a veiled dusk wet to the teeth
over vast tumour fields where injection phials are set down.
The herd gets its last meal, the straw's spread down,
next, sedation. The culler goes in
the bull taked out first. *'And you'd make sure, no matter how long it took*
to get close, that that was the next one to go. You'd leave the quiet ones
to the end. And once I started, I never stopped until it was over.'
Thousands of railway sleepers, tons of coal Acres of straw
a pyre built so chronically it burnt ten weeks
'Eight ewes we put in two rows on their side
on sleepers with heads of seven in the centre
and three lambs laid
over the ewes' heads.
Care was taken that the ewe bodies
   did not touch
     So that flame could pass around each carcass,
       a double layer of pallets was put over them
         & an 8 by 4 partikle load
           layed over the mass to deflect heat and flames to the pyre head.
It was intended that adjustments could be achieved by adding fuel
        beneath the crib & between the sleepers'

Wind unveils a Sediment
the white in smoke signifies flesh
maketh
fields peer flatter
    Saline in
      the cockerel water
          the pheasant
left pecking.

A depth field charged with a *ker ack of* shooting,
sieving out bodies in the light of psychopathic torches
edging to Darkness

I concentrate as blue lilies
wrap around my throat and blend me in hives for they are no longer
lilies but cattle placenta

Contiguous
Fencing
the motif birds of spring that make the song.
                Tomorrow
                      they *pre pep pre pep*
        nr abandoned straw some Trefoil
                on sheds & out into sky
black smoke in primeval fields
blood's oxide is moving to the outer edge of the surface
        not like the rings in the oak
        but under the rings of the oak;
                      blood drained from our cheek insides

Press your eye against mist shining gorse
sustained sunset on hills or hay blocks —
pious galvanise of water stagnant over field disorder
as you slip down *then you remember*
incremental glitter hit your eyes

you saw young men
walking abreast
pass you in their white sylph suits
down a lane packed with primroses
blood on their hands also their boots
across their stomachs then their collars

  'I met ghosts coming back from Ash Moor
who looked through me cradling udders in their arms'

In the coccooning month of May, shellac with spatters of acid,
corrosive resin on the domain.

Four cullers in white boiler suits at a farm, Monkokehampton —
jetting smoke in fields near Cadham
        A line of farms left and right of the hedge
                from Hatherleigh-Chulmleigh decimated
Between Morchard Bishop and Saint Boniface's the yellow JCBs —
        lines of coal

Fields riven, devoid of draught animals.
Daffodils. Solitary houses looking out
swans (2) a moot field to themselves
behind water-reed clusters

lanes are part bridge arching to the aether.
Rivers slop on fields.

Mist. Dead trees. Makeshift crop circles
Haphazard. Pylons. Dead sheep daubed in green Pentel.

    'Slap slap' on the narrow lane between spear shape hedges
the joggers in reflectors once so lustrous
the Countryside Alliance Young Farmers
Association Reverend Sabine Baring Gould affectionate afterhours
Society the wilderness of You Can Get Lost *below the clouds*
what the dead animals are is churned within the soil
   their flesh a rainbow of temperatures
      impotent owners at salted pyres draw cattle to death

'If I do not remember the, let my tongue cleve to the rofe of my mouth

As for our harpes, we hanged them up upon the trees

Then they that led us awaye captyve, required of us a songe

    and a melody in our hevynes'

then sat with silence crunching round their toes like King Size Tate & Lyle
when you see a maimed glint in the throat of the sky
you know the Okement and the Torridge are chocked with wreckage
on banks devoid of humans a polished sound
where canoes are set down by fleet footed ghosts, silent runners
where the

        sweetness I have come to sette
myself beside you with just one small song. Please hear it.
I am ever ready. Nothing gnaws me more than watching a dusk
sky fill with tangerine & white on April 5 and for a
while no other lights but spray
on the hills of flame folded in with grease freathing off corpses
the argent crescents these pious endstops

Orange sponge aisles in the fields below the squalls
greys & Blues in the low sky.
White rain, the neurological base of the
nervous system when spits of rain came in at Three One O per minute
as the sleep pattern clicks to snow behind the eyelids;
below star husks the endless cordite cordoned farms
talcum powder across fields burning a despoliation hymn

The Stars Have Broken In Pieces

for Roy Fisher and Joyce Halliday

On Ible there is
tang of wild garlic, delicious
and delicate – leavened with juice a longstem
gleam a white tarnish song

laving the coin of Derbyshire
keeping the brook shaded and white, turning the mill wheel
creaking the cam toward pixelated vista
in June the eve of Golden Bloomsday the peewit sang.

Rose haws dripped in sun spools the ferns
rank as finished coupling the breath
desultory this pristine guilt of having
taken pleasure; silent as the wheat cracks in sealed-out fields

heilio heilio the air like the road is steep
& the refrain is behind you, wet land slants
upwards full of flag and foxglove I began to think
of Stirling Moss decimating vultures in Panama

120 m.p.h., freathing carrion *heilio heilio*
Stirl's windshield & shoulders smeared in entrails.
'Ex-pyre', one field at Highflatts thick with straw cills.
By Piece Hall I dream of what it shall be like

when sun has gone far down, sweet mint dark
and in its position, yellow rape stinking : until the early
moonlight then our shadows reach and touch like
heraldic shields the undersides of wrists

and I will know and I will sing and spurt
and rail against the precision when love goes bad
and the harm gets done and xylophones glockenspiels eerie quiet
Peckinpah adrenaline until the silver line of dawn for birds

sluicing.

Running the tap
over the aconited lips the whirlpool eyes and mouth foam
your gaze silver and static when the
black is gone up to the red.

Some where on a road some where on a fork
a harepin a wishbone a skyline, going thru
the dark hoiking the anointed body
to Settle under the hawthorn below the yarrow.

Clouds are paling away from blue sky over Muker.
Carpets of RGB disinfectant exist until Tan Hill
and Reeth, then the dust of poppy petals on the road
the blue white and grey of mist, twelve miles in fog.

Threads of rabbits lie below gulls wailing
at cling film and flowers; roadside style – judicial,
mixed with dog corpse.

'You might like to be warned
of a bad character you would need
to avoid, twenty five years down the line.'

The stars have broken in pieces
you see sinews in the back
of the Archer, taut,
and with the stars the shoals the flocks
the intricate precision of *finism*
we know void-all about.

The stars-in-spasm
they lie with digitalis imprinted on their mica,
foxgloves of old, heavenly, Engeland
herds moving thru Settle,
                herds on jetties
glue on the heels of signatories
jelly falls from stars
cow hearts are tipped from a dawn helicopter
onto the pyre at Heddon on the Moor.

The stars are much of a sleat on my heart
on unsalvaged rooves loose branches and birds dangle
determine how the ear on incorrigible old
corrugate antiquity painted red earth hue
      the earth picks up the strains
yes how the heart travels and
the stars are much of a sleat on my ailing heart

The stars go down skime on the nub of the Okement, Devon
lying below the aura of the lightning & the raintorrent
where the cold otters are in pairs and the heron
is divided, half in the jolly sky from inexplicitude

and the heron's clumsiness is a tactic much like MAFF for accumulating
attack, the ear picks up information needles it through.
Information that has least service opposed to it
and the night goes thru and its bridge the recalcitrant stars

On Ash Moor there is salt sweat sheaved
                          below
the yellow filth jetty of marsh side temperance a throat harness
of silage unclaimed racked up to a previous year
the television is on but no one there sees it –

now animal hooves glitter erect in the full evening
spread against moors where they would unfurl flags next year
for the oncoming Queen   a full evening proud and gurgling
at the sun's dance of crushed harpoons

The stars get lodged in great jets of cloud
and with them goeth their spume their saline
ink and foil that unravels fissures of white -
both cloud and snow and see it is coming
cloud and sinew – hopeful constellar
      sleep and then the horses whinny
the Caterpillar crawls
and the trucks gather outside a farm. At 7am cullers arrive

The stars are much of a schour on my heart
or uncharnelled hooves loose breasts or tongues
hang decomposing to a glutinous mush
the scar of contiguous panelling
the pollen of human contact thru nostril & tonsil

the daub of foot and mouth fences
infinite caution the Do not Touch of motorway
service stations the Do not Touch because while we
may sell it it is likely contam-
inated and here the cherry reds of infection
blur with the brown and green fields
or hedges
the stars are much of a claim on my heart

Naked and free, naked and free
the lads are roaring stropped to the waist
on Scottswood Road, Heddon on the Wall
with no harvest.   Old valleys of the Tyne,
poppies, cowslips, glycerine roads

cuts in tarmac slice out pylons from the fells.
Tall lines, slender beeches. Robed graves, dressed wells,
shorn sheep. Popping gorse, big ditches; the capped driver knew
my nervous system was the merchandise
he was responsible for delivering.

From Mithroe Temple to Long Byre, past Burnt Wall Farm
a blue-toothed traveller stopped to pay a pub bill,
– last year's but not the year's before that, in one lump;
he left his collie strapped to a table as surety.

Today the railroad sleepers, the straw and coal
the granite of Richmondshire, snow poles
in County Durham; a ram knocks a curled horn
against a wall. At Kingwater the stream plashes,

kingcups over the green ironbridge, pupae to dust wedges
and rust coloured reflections of trees in water.
Flag irises, rhododendrons. Out of focus pine trees, lacking their bitmap,
alive only in geological time.

On the high land at Hartside
I took my bearings but let others look ahead,
now the heart's runnel was filling with saltbrine
the moated blood of interruption. The branched road was turning

among placards for 'Eden Limousine',
at Little Salkeld and Great Salkeld, tilled fields sharp
with weeds and white Scotch thistle;
the rain at Appleby cut sharp into hair
the horse fair cancelled

Pyrehic vistas, Eden Valley, thickly tree'd, peat cuttings brown
and green England's highest peak silent except bees & birds.
Tilled fields chocked with weeds. Edging the Borders
Bewcastle church sealed off with a plea

Newcastleton like the insides of a burned shoe
midges rework your face, the town's livestock
killed on a contiguous premise, information misconstrued.
At Longtown, past the Solway Moss
smoke rose, invoking the wailing of prayer

in the parishes of Arthuret and Kirkandrews.
They say the dead do not speak out; nor do they
move on as they pick against the petals
on railings. I have heard the trucks reversing

I hear the lorries turn, their stalls gleam
with blood below the yellow helicopters and gallivant birds,
it is finally true, candles have burned right down.

Very slowly drawn winched on tow lines creating tracks on
the beach you can walk beside the filthy boat blackened &
spat on by diesel throats & the sea's corridor of salt
Very slowly towed. Inebriate. And they are many, the Boats.
    handfuls of crabs are flickt onto the sand & our Gulls
who cruise at the Carny will take them down their gullets
What is wrong with The Crabs & Who would Ask This?
The men are mainly yellow   their hats are wool their collies skinny
or terriers, they waddle their heads misshapes. Baskets are set down
The trio walkt thru the black wooden cabins
away from the arc of the Boat beach away from gull leer

Scattered along they were many; the Boats were being winched
on the film lot
and the film will not be merry
The Boy who lived solely on the roof tops with the Gulls and
chimney pots satellite dishes
who was told Nver Darken are Door again
do not get Foot in our HOUSE *he lives like Mister Haw*
in a tent & in a hammock;!
his food zzooms up on a pulley
he sees what you do NOT see
<u>The Verey Old Woman</u> *dame*

The Very Old Woman who often lies down in the road.
Very-Tired. She falls over :
And the Boats are winching away
Upwards to the throat of the sand
The boat on the sand *: Goonight*

'Before Ivul' *Andrew Kötting*

Borzage

October.
Let the jelly of sky trace red soil,
sieve its stars through her spume. Night curves on a field,
your scarf curves your throat.
Your ribs jut thru' your back, your hands splay on the lens of night :
a bugle has joined a white owl in the pass and serve of a note.

Calling out is lonely, I know that.

Night has slowed down   beneath the quickening
stars. In deed night is a solace and a wonder.
The lonely outpost is revealed by a clear rake of stars.
Major Cleverdon will have plenty to say
about tonight's weather in
December's parish magazine.

Hedges silhouette their sharpened spears,
it is nearly 1 a.m. Our faces smart in the bonny air
but Major Cleverdon wouldn't understand *everything*.
Sky is teeming with stars; full, husked and embered
It is a beautiful night for setting out.

'I will hold my breath for a long time
and when I breathe out
another shooting star will be there. I will see it.'

'I've seen five. You saw only one.'
You walked together into the dark; lit by
the last of the lamps.   I saw
that look you sped across,   a fearful look of guilt and love;
a glance that became a gaze.

The Heron

A pale yellow moon on the horizon
sluicing through rushes of an ebbing vision,
evening raises and no human reconciles the hush
with what is ordained to ascend

the hush that is hurt from tumult of the agony
the wrenching of hearts from their shoals
silhouettes Hell among the Pleiades :
what makes you revile her for a decision you could not make?

A trade of every tumult,
despite every posit and rationale
a veering trade of abject weakness
in the silverine straw

And what was the decision that you made
when you would mount an image
spotted on bronze photographs to my face,
a gaze you captured, against a stone wall had vanished?

If it is speech that installs probability
and events that cause and crescend are upon us
and no notation's found
then is it not enough to subvert the image
iridescent of a moon radiant on the blossoms
that fell   when a shoreline changed   and insisted on a
heartless sickening time, time without polarity or edifice?

A pale yellow moon on the shoreline,
soil properties thread to eerie glitter direct
our footsteps, and words jut from horseblood earth,
the moon goes abroad sluicing fields
coating gorse with a pristine fluid.

>   The cold tumult
>   of winter is on your sleeves
>   you have decided on a whim
>   to go outside the parabola,

> I walk abroad with my conscience,
> yet I have nothing to tell you,
> I have admitted nothing
> because I must hurt you with scorn.

It was not the cold beat of your eyes that led me
to the Pleiades field to see a heron alight and sever her prey,
the gainless guile of the creature that could not hover;
I detailed nothing of the meetings I hid from you;
it was not the pasts we shared led me away from you
but the savage turn of your head, from all that is unreconciled

Lovers in a pleat of cockiness, we have exchanged our gifts,
and I caught the hush of limbs against mine
breath and laughter round lips meant for another man

I caught the sound of a conduit in abject sobriety :
a silhouette of a heron rears up between
our bodies when we are naked and unsated,
our sinews are taut when her hands are roving,

if I lie beside you it is not because I have asked you
to lie beside me, but because I cannot resist you

I saw the vision of a man at a public ordeal
with a rope thread round his neck
that would slowly loosen
cast from an upstairs landing

I saw a man weep because he was a traitor
and a child walking abroad in the hills
ablaze with phosphor; my bonny rosehip lipped lad.

Savage turns of the head
levelling out a lunar scythe
you breathe in the phosphor breathe in the lime
at a rapid shoreline

Every word you uttered made me suffer,
every silence I obeyed :
what was the use of all that gesture
and pain, I did not see the Reason in that.

I was not alone in telling you
that the word had spent itself,
the sound of your anguish
burns in my head

It was not the shame I shared that led me away from you
but a conviction that my dialogue was not solely with you;
and because 'I talk only of voices either real or virtual in my ear'
I went down to where the heron fed on cold air streams
and because it was dark, 'across a sepia estuary where I felt freedom' [1]

I could not see the heron supine on the shoreline
until I crouched down and Sirius was up;
not from its silhouette nor from reason could I find
a decision more painful to select

The ground lamp was turned to your face :
I saw you cry out and I knew your obvious rancour,
and if the coursing of blood
thru your blue veins could not be listened to
then I had no right to emote my anger.

My eyes were on the shore line
I could not determine the Reason
there was only the silhouette of branches at low tilt

freathed with spume from a river's gradience :
how could I admit to my heart
that I was wrong in denying a Passion
for a person I spoke wrongly to

that I was wrong in lodging an accord
to the person I had come to distress

that I was wrong in bringing a discord
to a woman I had denied truth to?

1, 2. 'The Heron', *Douglas Oliver.*

Sea Mortar

To walk the pitch of coast
and scrutinize Roy's Boys
fishers they cumen in
skittling the catch
to tar huts. A crew peer at old chapeaux their pay out

for a dismal day the coast is in melt down and the
Bonfire Boys host a Torch Jerwood party.   Tin glints
on the Arcade's sternum, below the blanche
of mortar,

when the deck chairs compensate for a winter
locked in a car park, so subterranean it's a
methane catacomb.

Air's stealth between sleeping rooms, strepsil sunlight
It had been dark and cold this morning and I
was melancholy to quit the spine of the sea
leave, leave again like unregarded mistletoe
my face pressed on ice cold glass
The grey pelt of water churns intestinal gâteaux
to adorn the English channel.

In the slope and sashay of the cinema
our chairs go down like decadent corn
below the scythe. On the jutting of the sea, Stooky Bill
dances a waltz with the glad Man who took a Flower in his Mouth.
We are all comrades here; and the man in the row
behind me watched his body turn to ash in
half an hour.
below the scythe.

'Step I,
you find some one and kiss,
step II, You kiss and hold her tightly. Sting croons in a garage
indifferent to custom, sending demo cassettes in faded ryvita packets.
Just what happened to the man overlooking the quarry
after he ascended the miniature railway
surrounded by gnomes? A man who has run out of caution ascends.
Just who is Jeff Keen? I will find out soon. Dream infront of Alexander
MacKendrick's *Maggie*; it, if memory it is, will all return.

And how does that reach, & is it all shot with sea,
an unripe lens on the Unmoving Café, where you walk past, texting
with salt on the side of your hands
your face watchful

The boy's ax poles the wood and a candle is put
between splinters to seduce a fire and
Roland Jarvis, animateur
is keen on a soupçon of pecharmant again.
He commiserates with all heirs of Calvin B. Marshall,
if they trust their cargo to MacTaggart's puffer *The Maggie*

But that was then; and today is today
as mortar recedes towards the alleys
sheltered from sea winds in broken yards and woesome sculleries
where 20 chair tops are propped and outdoor cisterns throb.

The sea rocks in and out as does the chain
levying a movement that occurs in corners
as soil seeps thru' sides of skirting boards
for slugs and wood lice to drag out the spring
ascent as high as the Toaster on the second floor.

Threading through the tableted cobbles, the
Winkle Club and Oxblood Arms once more
you scour the sea for a grain of pepper
to permeate coq au vin seared for Gervaise

Slow air   night and day   Undefiant
Echoes pummel the stomach
Sea light grinds against the glass. Diminish. Diminish

with no welcome for the coin of song
become eunuch a sawn-off-watering-can
as light recedes on the English way   (folkestone 33 m)

Vestiges of a yearning jostle me as I wake
when I fell asleep in the cinema; and the sea
reeds thru' my nostrils as if my body were a runnel
and I fall asleep again inured to quittance; ideas seeping out
like pared down wine –
the artifice of travel to Spain, Marlene and Cooper, dream of a diorama,
a wasp balancing on an Arrow of Grass?

The corners of this dwelling are cracked and sad. Insects thrive
on unusualness. See, they become animated
'Now they live in me as they do live in the ground'
Do away with parturition. Silent & Sombre
the very poor observe them. They will eat them.

There is a drizzle of poor from Folkestone,
and a promenade of suet climbs a skysweat over Bexhill
'I will eat calamares in the Old Town; I am old now and may not
attend a screening again. News has come in and receded, lined up
against the Marine restaurant.
I am not getting off at Ore.

A sleek of cloud is gathering on the sea at Rock a Nore.
The insects are trivial to you but not to me.
Now the insects live in me as they live in the ground.
I lie down and the sea cleans my lips
my teeth my ears.   Old parlance is echoed
thru' the sand stone   the cliff appears to walk
on stilts of chalk, and the dream I dream
is the breath you devour

"The wind curves slow fluid marks I can't read into surfaces.
I will be dust when I begin to understand the vibrations
conversing through me, between the rocks and the sea."

I gaze at the eye's internal pebble, your green eye
like a forest of moss at the base of the sea. But it is cold
it is sharp and the sea has framed her face
'It's cold in the train – I'm alone with the noise'

"Marks I leave will join with others.
They will record what has passed in a sentence
that stretches into infinity."

After 'Mortar' *Rebecca Marshall*

The Funeral of David Gascoyne

Wrapped in cotton wool each long finger
& every toe, around the navel & the nape
the face on a bed of finite filaments.
Tell me I do not know what day it is, I do not
really appreciate the month, I have been placed in the silt
just beside the window with a view upon a new cul de sac.
Outside there are acres of blue, pink, yellow cotton wool balls,
white but no black.

The clock here does not tick   the cat has stopped licking itself.
Although I care deeply, – feel such anxiety, for many people
– specially at this moment, I cannot face them & do not believe
I can see them. It is cold & I am quiet.
I used to be a schoolboy in a choir
that officiated at three state funerals. All a long time ago.

I remember holding your letter above me,
the rounded, squashed, blue characters
& "I had kept the sitting room exactly as
it was since that Sunday afternoon. The tea table
laid for nine people; 'taiga of sugar lumps
& carnations'."

"All we can do," it ran, "is enquire;
set up against the backdrop we've created
from our lives; & write these phrases down.
It may not add up to much. But rest assured,
it will inspire the true work that we shall do."

I see the most refined white you can picture,
succulent, it seems. Oh but it masks
& shields the despair you wake with;
nervous confusion,
apprehension. The feeling of being "of no use
to any one".

People & voices separate themselves
from me as to become humans & branches
… never quite discernible. At night I was woken

& offered to change rooms   where I resumed sleep
& thick with dreams; their information
of little use, but it cleared a path for the imagination
to somehow return to that backdrop.

The backdrop had now become a board
& on the board a rectangular tranche of blue wax
made my melting multiple candles.
There, somehow, I could begin to sit up & write,
stir & distil. I could not ascertain
exactly, what I could achieve by this.

The wind picked up its velocity as the day was ebbing
the blue becoming a white grey & I leaned out
from where I worked & opened my lungs
I could not presume to be missed. Not straightaway.

The Girl and the Dog

Grate the bitter chocolate
to that milk; the recipient
watches
with vegan eyes   *he looks familiar*

Cut the orange peel
place in the
sugar; stir with
vanille; pour over the crema

Along blue flame of the tent stove
I gaze at your wrists and face,
across the slow waltz of the spoon
I see the delicate ties on your shoulder

I am compelled to speak with you
because an arrow of sap is lodged behind my navel
You lean against a rack of low gas jets
your black hair lit by the parting sun

First there was a dog
then there came a child
that was the fact the melodia had
listen   but you are   latch
let me; *let me extend ladders to the moon*

we threw sponge balls
to the makebelieve
net you won 1   let me
rest your face on my fingertips
First her parents had a spaniel
second, came a dark haired girl

2

On the other face of her window ledge,
bairns flit past for school you lie asleep
and the dogs run against the surf
formed in the forests of their own perceptions

3

under the limbs I have barely scented
below the poised weight of your body
I listen to your musical voice
I think your hands are beautifully curved they are all bone
under your arms where I have lain
below your scuffed chin where I lean
to your throat, under the counterpane
below the stealth of your touch
quiet held in breathing
the fixed gaze
underneath our limbs

4

What does not want to be,
and what cannot be constrained, is,
and between the bodies of the dogs
lay a human ascertaining warmth
against the pelt against the mane, against the breath,
what does not speak, but is,
what cannot be deterrred, also is,
a world glued to the pavement
across the street, over to the pond,
where you and I lay, we listened
to the cat outside and the fly inside
to join the thrush of wrists, t shirts up, your delicate hands
'it is mandatory to eat; and drink' you whispered.
Rough terriers circle like rocking horse runners
Across the street, from the pond
where we did lie, we did listen
to a cat miaow, and the moth inside

5

Your face is a pattern of diagonals
her face in sleep
is twined with whom she does trust
your green eyes
your aerial cheekbones
precice nose   radiant lips
And dogs cough up the soil of their mornings
their ribs lamp out their exuberance
hand them out cut pear to counteract the salt
the foxshit between their hackles :
still there was a dog; a different dog
but also there were two

6

Behind the fluidity of your kiss
behind the almond in the eyes
or over the formation of a smile
there rests the diaphragm of motion
journey *eyes* adoration
And always in October this indigo dust
rises off the sloes
catapulted by the dog who chases the bird along the bough

7

I do not know why, you said, my dog
always barks at horses. But I
do not know why you said this half asleep
: it's getting cold, you said. We should keep walking ;)
The roads are dark
under your shoe, and streets
come away from them into
corner houses, a rounded chapel,
in the light you preferred, held
after sun had tipped; bright
colours splayed behind a hue, marbling each of
the pavements. There was first
a
dog, then there was a child

Sans Toit, Ni Loi

I thought I'd search
for her also. Vagabonde.
Just to say a thief is sly
      with another –
I saw them kissing also.
Gare de Marsailles.
  It was a roundabout way
of saying, No animal, crustacean,
invaded shore etcetera. Can't be done.
   Humans fix this game. They died upon her face
On the platform. She and that ravaged

The sleep you sleep is old with radishes
too small for Tante Lydie to chew
inside her cup of eau de vie
              and a white signpost
              below a plantain
              has torn down your name
    Mona
              none could be as lost as you;
must on your fingers and
fruits bruised black
      below your eye sockets

The broken mussels swirl on the flame
their awl of woad; she eats
he says 'Eat'
        at night on parched fields
her eye casts
over the moon's
mouth; her face is
beautiful disorder
but history
possesses an invasion
a mechanic's unappreciated
screwing
shingle   diesel   chèvre
what kind of (stomach freezed
waiting for a STOP) is that?

'He plagued me'

over the moon's mouth and
there is no moon
and no bone corridor
to moon and thrust
to sleep

The wind turns over the snow
    the dying vines
        the veins and fistulae of
            red earth, the arcs
 of a polytunnel
      scissored by snow
and in the snow a voice scalpeled
like gleam of bee wax
a voice knocks thru her hair
    throwing semi ice at her brow
the wind fans out the gorse and vine

Vines lost their
 best bloom
   in early
 frosts : petroleum blossom
now. In the townsquare her skin
had the wet gleam of flax.
Voices laughed through her hair
boys chucked hail and wine lees at her back
  her tobacco packet damp and flushed with snow
  and she in someone else's pageant
  lies with the lees like crosses on her face

Codeine sky and on it lights
    where the vine knocks
the stone, and inside the flat she'd said
"Assoun keep me warm" ——
   migrant workers drove her out.
     'The moon is a rough coin tonight.'

  The wind counts her death as Silence.
"I liked life before," she had said
"Before they told me what it was."

Poem

Pearls that were, her gentle slab
    suppurated by lime pollen oh gosh
those merry japes & veins that stood
    her gentle slab was kissed and tingled around the station
of Embankment against her throat a
    soothing balm look come this way into the
museum she said you'll never learn general
    knowledge else. Here she took
a bough of silence made steady her cause
    way and I promised not to look
at the boss of her eye I knew she told
    the truth so I promised not to look at the judder
of her heel her beauteous gazelle calf
    but ssh buba I'm going upstairs so place
your reading glasses on a straight nose and read while
    I sprawl in a vertever bath breathing in the flumes
of sidewayness : I cannot shake a drudge
of tambourine this big eared
gathering in our civic hall no leave the spots of the eyes
    to seal the niceties of straight
runnels of the thigh and over the fesse
    or between. It is a hard stair to climb
with gallowshumour and fortune favours the
    brave vanishing from the pittance
cloisters the eke conduits I assume
    you are brave and would have made a
fine nurse with your interest in the body
    and your vagaries of cleansing
your car don't buff the panels in the magenta
    sunlight just lay your soft head on
the leather and sip a lemonmade. I have been to
    the gallowspole and back just to wreak
havoc on my ancestors some of whom were
    slave traders. Today is a salient
bloom of capillaries. Intact I sip your lip of gin.

S.W.

Wings of making blood
the blood that is in your hair
gets
press of sideways finger
the blue harm in your stare
  Trace up to th' eye
   thrum on Adam's apple
Walk of pale
October   a rainglue
on Harts
hill oh yes svelte with black t shirt
levis   green silk shirt (grandmother's)
open
Walk of   so easy eye to eye
polite conversation   serve and pass
Score
a powder of firebrat
        a Minton alley tardis
Tempo   a heart pitched to a U –
            mag net
  Adjaecent lay
October 24.   meanwhile
                     in the warm lushes of Morleigh air
the upturned field arc
is malign copper

Quick body defined   Agile and so the circ
ulation in your long hands where secrets are,
how do you hope to bear an image or erect a montage
to cut across a road Circus without knowing turnings?

cobalt blue the haystream

Light picks out a bakery's cream ceiling
on the road a dog licks a post
two drabbers up from Cheadle to begin the day,
jaw and jaw, wind prowling with fishbone fists

That dolour of waking to see nothing beside my body
[distilling] gestation at the heart's font
quits the heath's rainbow silt of eyes
gorse flares under beeches   it is dark

a full countrie still deserted
an irrational argument in the street and I sleep alone.

To be able to do what you did by opting out
do what you wish   I want you still
Fairgrounds in Minton or Fresh Kills!
the ultimate adrenelin adventure
void-gone by March. Potteries, you could buy them now

horse hair clots my heart

all November, December grafters couldn't didn't
flog angelic toys what kids would want
possessions like that plagued sales screen dream teams
black cold knuckles lurchers eerie cots

Who has coasted a heart sledge
down a speedy hill, who knows without
pissing between the stones *which*
skyscape dragged a reflection

hung it one day out on gossamer bushes
one glorious May where the sounds of every stem
crackled on the sun law and every tree I saw
carried the ikon of hawthorn

blossom forced outside and stood necks bent
in the early morning wind, it was true and
then it was false the heart was polished
and lightly spun

Which stream, lane, that rill
doves' conduit, one channel to another
from Mow Cop where they might have walked,
could have walked trading favours

sensate just like a kiss on
the saving hill
the hotplate we jetted peanuts
just to see them spurt

with out a sun in the ear lobe
we knew it was dark and going to be just
ly so for a long cradling time

'til light would attach itself to the throat of
the church that caught the first sparks of
rain like a splinter in the heart
come off a corner in a Hansom

in 1903, all those undertows
a-way. Borne up in morning, scratching the skin
that made perfect a ductiling kiss
one plenish, one restock one open out splay
of loins / just to go where

the argent nit cannot reach but does
on the neck   warm hands
clasped one on other
on nape like loosing a string cannot get back

to shoelace, a good tie over leather
in a hunger sky scape dawn world
we lay there still we lay for the salt edge
of the fur that was far from the drenching

I would have liked

True as hands in horses the heart that leaves
a dandelion clock intact a sultry tang
horses past the satellite dish
dangling silver off a caravan

The slanting rain pioneers large petrol nooses up and
down a road. Hyacinth rissoles, eerie outspent wild garden pools
not the no, and not the yes To get incredulity at absence :
glow worms, rooks, eel legionnaires you didn't see

Swallowing beers,
one for each preferred Side
of the moon / The Pleiades
are low
And now night. el Side Car. Vide. Cerrado

five rooms reeking of butterflies,
  a zebra with extended dick
reams an engorged male and ejaculates.
Got your money for a hotplate,   a kettle, why fill it?

None to watch, no nobody
nul to care for through Sleep's sieve but you do not
sleep my delectable One no no stomach to slide hand over
your ear to kiss your loins open for kissing, your lobes alert

tell me you prefer waking bright and rosy
to the solitude of sluicing alone
in a night with no coin to lob into a jar
let dioxin rain lead you to Queen Anne Street and disown you

In the quarry over the brow
the hill from Longnor I
find the sill on, the rawing curves of terraces
like an orange past its sell-by

date this was the exposed side of the moors
where'd ya like a ladder stacked up? the eaves or the Joists
I mean I've got [a] work to do?

lining bitumen just a smi'gen
an' keaping the rain from bleeding the house
out of its spine, this is a world 'as needs
restoring, out in the roof-tops down in the foundations

A rose branch has gone to dust
the large vat of Silence Still
the glade
of fractured Summertime

Oh heroine /// the words reveal themselves and place our
actions, reveal our actions by our words. (*John Wieners*)
The silence of lovers
     hearing Townes Van Zandt sing
black crow's in the meadow   off a broad highway
past meadow rank with lopped spines
of narcissi   my heart has gone to Nomansland a
     carbon
pose, a scarlet
wound. Break up the dust
of your envelope, it won't
matter much, scatter it
and cut lightbulbs
in your hands
     and every body will be
chipper tonight
with sluices on full pitch at the zenith
    and the moon shining on broken bedboards
and the reel my fingers danced in your black hair my dear head
I didn't think of consequence
     I didn't request your lenience
the sun went up on Leman Street
the sun did thread through couping the wolves' willow jaws
      and I would be leaving in a while

the sun did harry Leman Street
carried on down to Queen Anne Street
   A fishing craft
waves foam thru waters
     as sea's always trinkets
       they seek in waves and that's a useless pulse
To expose my ribs to sun light up (remember)

yes I need a get-out of this hap
hazard milkbottle top in
the nervous sysytem maiming.

There is a shell in the loins
which grows inguine To tide you over
she says I'll place you on my other side

but you'll be near the door and to the draught
it will be fun to spend these 9
days with you, mainly screwing, walking but
some eating

The yearning smotes of silencing kisses
just over the forehead near th'
eye   would you   have said you waited
a long time   for this? I mean weighted
waited S'all the same

LISTENING TO THE STONES

Poems of New Caledonia

For the family and the life we shared

A Noumea, le journal d'information de 18h30 de Radio DJIIDO qui faisait une large place aux évênements de TIETI et à l'heur historique, a été démocratiquement brouillé. Ce soir c'est l'ensemble du Peuple Kanak qui a le sentiment d'être pris en ôtage dans son pays occupé.

Bwenando numero 104/105 [Le Premier Journal De Kanaky]

Prefatory Note

New Caledonia is an island in the South West Pacific, and is an Overseas Territory of France. It is part of the Melanesean region which includes Papua New Guinea, the Solomon Islands and Vanuatu.
The title of the book *Listening to the Stones* came from an interview Marguerite Yourcenar gave in *Le Monde* in April 1987.

R.S.V.P. Edward Thomas

Luck took charms from the wreckage
of two summer cars – their chassis
so long marbled in the woods companioned
by the careless rout of birds

strange to find them there,
you'd pass lightly through the wood,
the marsh with a scented mantle of high flowers
where rats fought for bread in elephant grass.

Yes you'd have walked; out and away
from the wood, only to return after watching
leaves climb the sky – to take from the yellow car
a handkerchief, an invitation card.

Your grey eyes flecked by orange pith
scan the invitation card, its map weathered
in lilac ink; sunlight stung your temple,
you have sanely followed this route

        –   –

There was a large house, bay windows open
onto summer, you stood on a verandah
shy of voices fading,
blue butterflies dropping onto faces.

At last you walked into the lush grass.
For a second. Sky became a fever
of purple yellow sponges torrenting on the lawn.
Those who touched them vanished.

Petered out into the dark. In the hot
light. You never saw them again
and they never saw you. Reflective
cupped hands tracing a silver stream.

                                          12-18th March 1988

The hour of escape, a delicious state
of spitting out lilac : I dressed, undressed
then pulled on my shirt etcetera
hearing sound three leopards make   hunting fowl
on another continent

I have not forgotten your hands of water reed
becoming reed, as you rinsed them in the brackish
river. Your head curved and beautiful at the last moment

a tree

split open from the silt of a potato field.

Here, these are green wet leaves. Do you take my kisses?

Towards the white quai of geese, von Sternbergesque
market garden huts. Today Nijinsky is so
in my mind that I inexplicably
link him to the dearest garden of ....

Dark the sky, like the final drops of wine,
purple rooves gleam for   a final denial
of inertia. They say a thousand seconds die in the dawn.
Geese squat by gargantuan puddles,
then I loved, loved immeasurably everything

December 31st, 1987

A Holiday

White heat pulsed in the natural clock, the worn
-away sand filled linear as thatch
by fleshless wood. Ridges of straw
burn on th*e cases*. Rooves
of liverish tin, seaslug thresholds in the low sea :
crabs minute as your nostrils scuttle, butterflies
calendar the clouds. The ocean paused
in a braid of rays. At Mahamata I
remembered the bodies of cattle after the flood
the brindle pelts on the scum. There we were
not voyaging to the ocean at all
but on a vehicle raft crossing up
from the estuary, in the valley to Hienghène

A bar on the state road, pass
    the soft-drinks hatch to a garden of
Number Ones, chicken earth. Papaya swells
    over moustiques entranced by bird entrails.
The bar unlit, quiet. We were nearly
out of diesel. Whitefolk had quit Balade
Hienghène and Tao
Houialou Ponérihouen   Pouébo.
    KANAKS blew up the petrol pumps.

When we asked where to buy diesel nobody spoke.
People's ears were leaves.

Abattoir cool
over the bay, Hienghène gendarmerie,
the cops strapping surfboards to their car
didn't reply. To get diesel
we asked in fourteen places. Miraculously a Vietnamese
    leading two ponies points to a river bank,
we cross with a can.
We pass the army camp's
honeyed filets of wire : a soldier in caleçon points
his rifle at us, bored by
    the Pacific. To a house wrenched out in a cyclone
we arrive; foundations jut like horse teeth

    where a master lived, who has now gone.
Gone with the dead, gone with the spilt,
    gone with the flags, gone with the current.

In a shed flanked by tabou leaves
    under peachjuice of the sky
far from the shacks parching in mangroves
    a toothless vieux in a Sid Vicious t shirt puts a tube to our can

Sun draws through rain, the whorled hills
gleam with jacinthe; we rise over Hienghène, town-of-the-dead
the low ocean tramelled in all their green scarves.
Niaoulis sway on dust tracks, dusk
in the warm rain a crystalline hush

The Pathways of Guava

Along terraces to a precipice
blowing with water hyacinth
lit by a grey boat
a heron soars from stones
to tree, he is the king of birds
and holds in his slow unfolding wings
the horizon of the waterfall
where he will be disguised as a plant

Of country stars
encountering space
before dawn☐closing petal   we are
no nearer a path that spoke
a sentence when a stone curved
over to say no doubt your eyes
were imaged in ashes of a
fire struck out in a cave :

We reached the mountain cap
at night's frail, the pinks
of the pools drew sleep
to our eyes; a goat's bleat
pierced a path we crossed
at hush of dawn ─────────
       spiders wove their graphs
       of blood, a queen searched for
       the white ball of her eggs
       tumbled from threads on dew
       wept by the crow blind so soon

Rocks plundered earth
dreaming their genesis,
dawn rose on a cross
carved in the petroglyph.
Goats clattered on the stones.
Silent whirlpools of rock
follow the coin and forget the coin
the coin of stone I drop

─────────

Here are terraces to a precipice,
the labyrinths
of sound, stone.
You saw .. four knife lines
for a face consecrated
in stone – a skeleton
coiled in shale

In the rejuvenescence of the mist
stones lean towards stone
roofing moist shale, sun swims
a white path beyond the mountain peak

It is little more than five hundred years ago
that people first visited the sea.
And with the sealevel dwellers
they bartered shells for leather;
knives for custard apples

We drink tea from a jar.
The wind below the sun threw
the sand at leaves, the dogs parted the bushes
for us, leaving the shore garden. Twilight

---

in the bay where cattle sleep,
turtles bury eggs, yellow tricot rayés
flicker through the water's long hair :
see, the cabling drift of sand
lanes of webbed seagrass,
a treefern a gigantic séance point
lookout occasional kingfisher,
onyx sandgrains falling to sea :
of country stars
encountering time
before each dawn, of a bouyant soul
a closing petal in the ear, tell
nothing, tell no one – .. of the
woman walking in the sky
that leads us all to stations,
tramping in the seventy-sixth year.
Sunlight combs Maria's white hair,
her dark skull : water walks
over rocks smooth like

brontosaurus eggs,
you listen, you listen to the stones ...

Lodged in her shack
behind the green paths of geckoes
in between two walls is a basket
of monnaie Kanak that will be taken from you
now you are widowed

You have to
         leave
there's nobody
    to be at peace with
you have to leave this fragrant world
in the silence guavas give to death.

You will be driven here or there
your sinewed legs under a flowered mission dress,
under stars that gleam as they arc for your
heart

Summer in Dream

The fish sped by eating at its

gills, opaque leaves floated ...
    Summer. Joyous mornings

a country in your dark emblem of hunger,
rainsoak rooves : implications screen fear
from Caldoche cowboys who pursue geckoes with an electric scythe

Ballade, Poindimie, I saw dead blue-dogs in the sludge of the river
in whorls where it stang your eyes to see the fur

I saw a dead pony licking a ladder
I saw a forest that was all on fire
she saw a girl frozen in the gutters of nitrate

– You who swore as you watched so many suns rise
—— Unfathomable reflections in sequences of water
drunk deep in the lengths of torture
        fishing fleets receded from the vortex :
downstairs nothing could be heard but footsteps of assassins.
You who search for the white beaches dreams the estuaries have receded
And listen to the chink of nickel in cut glasses
still have not encountered the miraculous unadventured in colour

Softly closes the gate at Churinette's.
It is October again, and in the hills
many houses are without floorboards. No requirement.
Flags portray portents.

The side gate ajar
Tarnation at the hostels
Endless kettles, endless ridiculed lives.
Lizards, finches and jacinthe among the weeds.
Old songs are never themselves again
in dilapidated cabanes : lakes in embassy gardens
dazzle with stars, streams
flow under plantations of tribus
their locked in luminance

The cold afternoon glistens around the lake.
The flesh of rabbit, goose and papaya
hums on the grate. C.R.S. march thru the planetrees
kicking sand toward the campfires.

Although barely a stranger, I, for one did not know you.
The flashes in the evening were harsh and lingering.
The lit yellow wing of our batch
under rainbows silhouetting the sheer intermittent gullies

In crystalline weathers
we walked
our hands cupped
these moving lips
did the pass and serve
of lovers' talk
persistently gave them
truth of process and gliding unity?

Studiously we found a monument
Laid on the vista thousands of years ago
Flint upon flint scored into a giant with hands outstretched
Rose across the pervenche skies
like whips into corn
and we descended from Pueuo, legs wet
back home through white spears of niaoulis

For Louis Tjibaou, Sculptor

White heat pulsed in the natural clock, the worn-
away sand filled linear as thatch
by fleshy twigs, landcrabs tiny as your nostril :
heat pulsed, and there we were not directly
at all with the sea, but going somewhere
inland, a raft and towrope bore us

And had passed, a nerve in the human spring,
past erosion, to the poles of this summer wall
(a settlement)
night drank down to seacaves, eel lantern lit :
Louis Tjibaou was the champion
and between numerous dusks and dawns
time travelled ahead finding sea water identical
but dropped down with shadows of nine other
tribu men bound to die

Three men walked in discourse
– to grasp work from thought –
cold wind slung the bell
shading a church tower, light scores
masons' faces by static wheelbarrows

After the Festival 2000
Kanaks on stilts wearing white capes and gendarme hats
ridiculed the legislation

past violet blue bushes and to a table
(a pen of sleeping deer threading their reflection)
Louis Tjibaou, a sculptor scribbled the plan for a church
in the rotten dawn. Blue shovels dug warm earth. Treetrunks
cut, quartered, the First Church
glistened here, a painted tin roof; for worship compelled
us and we saw stained glass in the paint

And had passed so lovingly, the light.
Grew green and taller than a mountainous
path of no beginning nor end,
time travelled ahead to where men's shadows would die
leaving the road free to a frogpool, the noise;
a faceless franju woman walked down past

A moment sealed with cottonwool dawn, light moored
its seal.
Atoms imperative to existence.
Sky seals no more sky than's
necessary; and the warm sea, seaslugs,
tricot rayés ferns black rock anemones
wash together ... now the sea's volume fills

Columnar pines
liana
the geckoes speculate

            ... And the road paused
in its braid of heat.   So that ....
Louis curved like a sickle into unknown ferns

and walked upriver over the stones   jumping angular
curving around tall banks and boulders, between
creepers till reaching the plinth of the waterfall
where rock curved smooth russet into itself, you dived naked
into the pool

II

You return by the same path
not wishing to return,
expecting a signal
            under clouds that fall
like peachjuice

you looked again
at fascimiles of civilisation
increased straits of greening sea
– clouds pull to the amber horizon
gulches, false tributaries formed by cyclones,
the sea. Sagaille fishers. Knelt.
Finally you come to pray

                                      February 17th, 1988

III

Pitted by cattle hooves soil froths
in the cup of the river, in a stained peach hat
Atelmo Taufiferiva stoops in the tall grass
feeding green pigeons to the eels

Pause

A new evening

Now you walk below

overripe acajou trees : link my hand in yours
pressed to your lips. Of all of your questioning body
your spine's a mahogany branch
in the dusk of love's sweet presence

The river curves through the shadows green
by white trees and all too soon we have
met winter, eroded in the hands
of Canaque fishermen

Hienghène

Trumpet snouts of piglets fossick
earth lit by banana peel, sow's ear
catches on wire – a gap where her young
have sprung to grub up snails
among blue bread and pumpkin rinds ———
light glades light on the ridge
in Hienghène valley.
Hooded Kanak vigilantes
sort out guns, whistles of torchlight
under a flèche fatière. Stalactites hang from moon;
centennial eels unfurl on the pool floor, out of delicate silks
moths swarm to fertile dressing plains, to dull radiance
framing a *case,* weaving thru a flèche fatière.
Valleys have swum to the moon to disappear, rivers still thrive
but the moon's milk is rancid,
moths take away the sleep with them

cicadas steal
    birds voices
        instruct deliberate our ear,
the frogs pretend they're abroad and
you listen to them croak, they in darkness
have you assume forests are moveable,
the intermittent sound is that of nesting birds imitated;
to the chill of the frogs the forest turns its ear,
noise goes thisaway, you hear the frogs have moved again

A woman presses aspects of her husband's clothing,
a death globe in her wrist.
                              He has gone, Louis.
He will return.
Given unto his pulse sixteen cheeks of children
this cocotier leaf bed, your hour.

An old woman whose russet beauty
is stitched like leather, complains of the tribes,
she worries it will rain on the oven stones :
a flourish of cattle jolt on the banks

then guard the waterpath that you like a warrior
should not flinch

In an inlet of the sea
      she checks her seine
           it is calm here, with the cattle
An unhurried woman, too tired to walk
closes her eyes waiting by the ocean.

Turquoise of the waves
      sky is floating out ....!
two corners from the bay landcrabs are all hidden
in the sand

The seines are checked.
Below the Magellanic clouds
inlet tides suck upwards, seines along the estuary
weighted down in sand and weed;
waves bend ashore, raise sand in their spines :
a causeway of green écume casts the spirits of ten bodies
exhumed from the river out to the wind across the stones.

The eye's corner snaps heat it can't reproduce.
Watch the rise and fall of time, follow kingfisher
heraldic thru Tiendenite valley. A blowing cactus flower
scurries up a highway
pungent in frogs on shoehorns.
Cached in a white sack opposite the gendarmerie
five chickens claw for a horsey head.

The heat rolls over the gendarmerie roof,
yellowing a white surfboard propped
against a truck; breeze is lit with salt
coming from the ocean. A plane touches down
a helicopter goes, envoys and emissaries. Enemies and pawns.

Blue cattledogs listen to laughter of the stars
on the stones in blanche archipelagos
teeming with chrysalids.
Out of delicate silks moths swarm
to fertile dressing plains,
swim towards the moon, to be taken

by the sea current … tonight moon's lait is left out and rancid
Tabou leaves shimmer, lint to the tribu. F.L.N.K.S. flags hang
off arucaria, roads in Northern latitudes pitted
with wire and treetrunks till Independence's gained.

Brooding fever speech
unthreads leaves of the tribu
chases away the grandparents' eels.
Cherry-hued eyes close,
effluence of crushed snails
is thick on the sleepwalking stones.
They fear rain on hot oven stones.

Radios announce all day
"Kanaks are killing metros, burning properties
(soon our journalists will interview the champions of Hienghène)"
spinning words of wool between each tooth
don't trust French journos who came
brushing away chicken bones

six bec-de-cane on a fisher's shaft are dropped
when a vigilante hides from the spies : sway tabou leaves, shield
their land the roads will stay
pitted with treetrunks and wire
until they get Independence

In Nouméa Caldoche and Front Nationale schemed
to assassinate the Kanak president,
hatred glowed in eyes and lungs
of people grouping to slaughter neighbours
in lush hills, green with chaotic birth. Death globes
rest on their leathered wrists. An old man this humid night
what did he speak of but how footballs are made of blood, and light planes,
you believed him drunk in the valley
reciting in his warm white head
from the Book of Job. A heron flew from stone to stone, distracted
by the spell of seconds she swam
to the sky. 'There'd be so quickly ten dead,' he said.
A December moon is rising over New Caledonia.
The moon rises over Hienghène past.
The moon is lighting the bushes sapphire

threading shells on sunlight. Over the church
moon glowed on the hand-painted tin roof.

And had passed so lovingly, the light.
Grew over niaoulis like splashes of lightning :
colours of peach this dawn in the sunlight,
crossing poles of the summerwall.
Louis Tjibaou lined up the chairs
for the meeting, and this evening the clans came, masses
with banners voted to move the barricades. A truce.

The moonlight crossed the stones of the summer wall
Tonight they came from Hienghène valley
came and went from Hienghène present; in two battered trucks
sharing a headlamp drove seventeen men needing supper,
seventeen going home, the night Lafleur engineered.

A portion of meat twitched
in his ear, his cock stuck out for a fleur de lys
a squirming shadow of death Jacques Lafleur prescribed.
Dawn would wake the engineers of this massacre
to fill their eyes with dead men's dirt —
men because they carry Winchester rifles, métis
farmers in wide death linened hatbrims
riders possessing knowledge of the unborn dead
inside the stag carcass, the pig entrails,
sharing out blonde cigarettes.
Caldoche women and men aiming rifles delivered by helicopter
who knew how the light gapes from a broken back;
trampling moonlight, knotting rope to coco palm, Raoul Lapetite
his four sons ploughing blood in the soil,
it was time to crack laws into powder between their knuckles.

Eerie silence tunnelled from the moon,
there was a stagnant wrap of dynamite,
asphalt became sticky with mangoes, hot coco palm glued the road;
the explosion blew the two trucks together, melting and
interlocking them : from shadows came neighbours to Hienghène tribu
supplied in the city with rifles,
toothlike in the smoke to build a podium
wet and bloodied around the trucks,
torches and alsations maiming the river

tonguing cushions of blood. Slumped but not dead in a truck
with his 21 years Lucien Couhia
slumped over his smashed arm gazing at the frame of a friend
preoccupied with his space between the wheel
and the door. Light hangs like a perverted censer over the bank
where grass was falling from the eyes of a man flung
behind a path moistening the iridescent soil of sun   where
the large wounded needle of his death
lit a shallow line of water. Caldoche despatched 2000 cartridges
that night, they set live bodies alight.

The night Lafleur contrived, the night witnessed
dead Mandjia in the larvæ of the river
his weals where Maepas' eyes stung to see the sand
pour from his thighs, saw one living today
lose his testicles, and one escape treading on bodies
saw a dead man licking a ladder,
saw a truck that was all on fire.
The moon saw a young man bloodied in crevices of fruit
she saw a machette fall on the eyes of an old man.
I saw a world where music had no origin
I saw a tree weep for Tarcisse was burning

The sap in the soil that may sponge a body
and square out the blood is disturbed
by cockerels that crow; and everyone has
dashed an extra fist on their nipple
without wishing it so; mucking their hearts with sirop
and the children do not know whether to cry
more with their mothers or by themselves. Children's tears
are blue butterflies on the riverbank,
the singular visit of pain, the doubting of behaviour
the cutting of a language the tears crying out loud where's my father?

Children are on their pillows or below the lightbulbs
clogged with death – with death that is not
preoccupied with dark, but with light
that is moonlight vomiting on men's faces

The cold bow of fish sped through the shadows
of water among the leaves, and the light
hung like white creeper around the still form

of a body scored clean by water. Grain
spilt from his lips.   Sunlight, froth, whistle, dance !
Ax heat grinds. A group of children
flown in the rain, the state of France, the schools are boycotted now.
No longer swallow they your history your flowers of the Ardèche
Four tall green pillars on a faraway horizon,
          columnar pines mark the tribu land
remember the mouth's spat green

Louis' body lay too open to sunlight
for dressing; it was dead anyway and not like a body.

When the women pulled
Tjibaou's body to rest
     on the burned out truck
they found another there
    a third heron soared over the fleuve
        Human would fly like that if
flights were
    rejuvenance
but that cannot be now

Women of the tribu
saw men on the river's other appel
inbetween the trees
who took so long to speak.
The group of women got to the hill,
the wall has collapsed, the cord snapped,
fishes are scattered, their heads in all directions

She, Céline Tjibaou
misunderstood the raised hand
'I did not look : or maybe
forgot what a sign like that
would mean' when she found her husband
stripped to the hips and broken over
where a t shirt had been
'If these were your husbands
we would cry for you, we cry
because we are women : I don't know,
maybe we will see clearly together.'

In the pasture of blood there lay a man burned to a tar soap
and under a tree knelt a man spooned out
to pawpaw : the women of Hienghène laid their clothes
down on them, down on the ten.

Twentyfive mynah birds on the mud sore road,
a quicksilver flock the illusion
caused by sunlight; today temporarily
birds halt the sumer wall of traffic,
at one point to go in single file
you undid the mirrors to your cars :
so went the voice that none could claim
in the shrimpnet silence passed down the bus aisle
that ten were dead, dead at Hienghène.
A paying of homage, a giving of digestion
to do with cicada larvæ the bright
underwings flurried like mission clothes
twenty five mynah birds for one of their own
crushed like a hairbrush on the road.

And out of the distressed mosaics of faces,
of black faces, those of Albino gardeners
in the sweat bowers of their seats
came the knocking sound of rage; in the hot day
nothing moved on the brows of the huts!
The silence of the grandmother's forearm
presiding by the dusty window was the burnished shadow
of her dead son who'd passed parched out of the night.

February 1988 – May 1990

Note – In October 1987 the seven *Caldoche* (descendants of the original settlers from France who openly confessed to killing unarmed Melaneseans on grounds that, be,cause the Territory was in a state of civil unrest, they acted in self-defence) were found innocent of any crime. Amongst those acquitted were Raoul Lapetite and his four sons. In April 1988 Raoul was kidnapped from a farm in Voh. On the same day his son José was found shot dead on the farm.
Jean Marie Tjibaou, a former Jesuit priest, poet and president of the FLNKS (Front de Liberation Nationale Kanak et Socialiste) was not among the ambushed party. Two of his brothers were among the dead. On the island of Ouvea, on May 4 1989, Tjibaou was shot dead in a political killing.

Dawn

Blue dawn she rouses boats in a harbour,
tarpaulin and flamenco squid waken. Mass she gives
to ink eyes and self poisonous scales,
seines drag through water to ice-chocked casques

… beside a bramble feast in the first wood I
caught Love by the ankles and laughed.
We turned a bed from wild raspberry straits

Because a cow was slaughtered and the guts pulled out
and a snot-caked girl tunnelled up the carcass, stood inside,
emerged to drink milk from a hacked-off teat, for this

I heaped bamboo at the gate, to hide further rites!
I climbed high to young fields ashamed of my colour,
found a place to sleep … alone a few hours

The moon was starting to hide, cattle like chess pieces
chewed white grass. Horses cantered
erect through the forest, the river sang. While I slept
the apothecary the l'Indo Suez the supermarché ransacked
all filing systems immolated

January 30th 1988

I Dreamed I Dream : Ouvéa
The trees whistle, the sun carried out the bodies of nineteen men

Luscious wind   opaled grass
soil spilt from rainbows pursuing sagaies,
sharp prongs kids piercing thru fish :
nasses trail across weed
   riven backwards with the pincer slash
of lobster
river curls to pool

It is moonlight, and niaoulis
on fallen blue earth POINT
N.N.W. :   lunettes fly fly
a chest span of thicket away
      –

shall always be moonlight a younger world
North, you get the best hard ons
or juiced up at the same crevasse each month,
   frequently alone

Behind thick flushes
of spiderweb Death
by a marginal fishing bay unforgiven
on a Friday grassblades crossed
in water meadow, fish dried under television sun
over coconut oil, moustaches of fire
red below skillet – a day resonance broke

down along Eastern paths
cutting in and out from sea, when the sun
hauled out oranges. A vallée one winter
lost each blossom

In tennis courts the C.R.S.
imitate geese, and when the game is won
they drive to hotels to dream of pâté
How deserved their pay! how do you love their instruments of lethality,
tambourines they conceal in their pockets?
   This silent war to keep a colony's fresh
out of its shoes.

A tapeworm crawls out
looking for the eye in a can opener
light on a coconut brow
a head rises below a plough
ing of day stars, dawoua swept by tide,
knuckles raised up like rope —dice men spun
through light that shared same fissure
a genital needle of death, ax
and bushknife underwrist
O my dawn swelled like my blessure to the atoll
when in night of the sleep of a tide
a head rose from a pillow of wood;
then three gendarmes lay
hacked up to sacks of mollasse

high windows open onto sunlight
            fresh scythed grass, concurrent to the plain
follow how you are coaxed – musical patterning splayed in the head
sky filled with indigo yellow partikles
darkening the paddock
In the hot air   whosoever   touched   the   partikles
evaporated   –   I watched cupped hands passing through a white stream
beating foam along the rocks
                I dreamed I had washed in death
                where no one could be more part of the
                            stream than be buried in it
                I dreamed I followed a voice
in the green light among the traffic, overtaking wrecks
on bends in dips I glanced at my neighbour's pages
on the Noumea-Tiendenite *Sunset* bus

He read from the Book of Job :
white larvæ engrained in flesh
   of Tiendenite valley dead.
Indigo faces serene in r.e.m. voyage
   moths participated in thrumming a yellow luminance
on ciel; I did not expect to see purple water hyacinths
growing   March 25 / from the wounded window
on the bus   radio playing Eagles
Sun will set then light turquoise domaines
or seas shall pull and thresh up stars
left for lord knows who on each shore

slow shall be the scrape of worse than metal
the tree of mourning flung in the ocean,
a body that is purple turn to fruit,
fishing nets plein of blood, trailing marrow into vertebræ

remember now, Montage
of scarlet sky; night and sloshing waves, a chapel freaked with geckoes
Man of Peace, a howl fills the sea : the moon returned to the shores
of Ouvéa. Waves crack on the atoll.

Shoes were scattered about the sand, sand with the dead
sand for the dead who share burnt kettles, blue bread with new sunlight
showing the living NOTHING
but death in the nape
of spotlight.
A teaboy's corpse flung in a bush beside bust tubes of an intravenous :
France is asleep with piss in her mouth.

Tall trees whistle, the sun does carry
   out the bodies of nineteen men :
how do you equate *sacré* with mass /
sacré ? a breeze sending Séraphin's body
   out to sea shells

Prayer

In memory Jean Marie Tjibaou, president F.L.N.K.S., Yeiwène Yeiwène, his deputy president, murdered on the 5th May, 1989 by Djubelly Weà, at a service commemorating the 19 Kanak separatists murdered by French G.I.G.N. forces, the Onzième Choc, etc. Some separatists were executed after surrender, on May 5, 1988 on the island of Ouvéa

>They have taken the lion
>to the oldest fairground
>in pools of blood   below helicopter skis
>Jean Marie Tjibaou and Yeiwène Yeiwène dead as it gets
>
>'Without words our ancestors showed us
>–   to fling the tree of mourning
>–   to the river's sprain
>
>It is time for all of us to hurl
>   from our hearts the trees of dissent' :
>the purple of our sternums turns to fruit.
>Moon spits into our deer's antlers.
>
>We light sticks under sky
>we hurl branch-first, the tree of dissolution :
>fire culls all hate.
>The cross is a path a man waited on.
>
>Cill of our *futur* over the ashes' paths
>must be cut through in the lunettes'
>clear-song.   I know the lunette always flies
>to the next bush as we advance.
>
>Communion. Poise of thought.
>   Out of trees that grow
>   from dew the circle overlaps the cross
>   in pools of twilight on the rain fields

freely adapted from Jean Marie Tjibaou's poetry
March 23rd 1988

At night the sleeping rain
sieves a marble valley
the breeze's shoal and creatures' sinuous paws,
eyes of almond dazzle white grass

                                                March 26th, 1988

The Difference between Sunlight and a Wedding in Pothée

Scented tides of rain
and flange of fern
      below a wind spray of mist
encircling each rock : in the heartbeat

      at morning a fleet of creepers are hanging for a dual rainbow
. I woke up. Counted 7 hills.
At the rainbanks of our frothing river
below pink trees and white trumpet flowers –
there are sharp pits where horses did pass.

The word, 'morning' –
to think of it, o purely
the 7 hill length of it
to wake in that gold emerald light.

How soon the valleys become marble
sunheaps; fresh hiccupings
of unshared fruit pervade; on the river side
you see cicada shells.

This morning three Canaques are waistdeep
leaving the fleuve; fish threaded to the shaft of one man's sagaille

A stream threads toward
the threshold of the paddock, to the breeze :
a vagrant doll of love floats on the
silver water   What's this? a shout?
it's only   peace breaking out

In the stillness of the corn
mice cavort over bows and wilting darts
In the swaying of the corn
spiders search out the spider's aluminium throne

The wood turner said he'd return to Kenya,
I was pouring him coffee, he was asleep,
later we walked across blossoms of the rain
to his car and drove up the banya road

This was the first road the prisoners built,
the banks of parched bread earth
split the forest, the road mesmerised by the hills' cones

You told me the tale of the cyclone,
russet hectares of smashed frogs, yolks of chickies
herons dipped to eat, picking through the niaoulis
at the chain of drowned engineers.

A lush rain on our shins, lips round the yellow oval
of tobacco we watch the crates loaded : a
banquet of beer,
rice frails, inyam, taro, goat.

And here we walked out, into the shade
and tilted our hats back
      looking at the red whorls of teething
brick in spate over the chapel

          Not a rainbow !
      but a vitraux of 7 colours in the shells
of sky, of wedding,
in clouds haring to Pothée

The Air Is on Fire

Air breathing over flèches fatières an auerola to pliant saplings and shadows
and the murals fading behind the spray paint in colonial houses
The white shells of theft where air falls and swims like a music
Look ribbons of light pinned to the struts the jug of
windows where glass was filched and began to sell at Bourail market.
Air breathing over the eels' sleep path, an aureloa to blossom and reflections
pursuing the coppered rays for elusive moments of air in water
the life like eyesight's renewal between each dualation of water.
After pricking your ears with a whisper
via the resin your blood created in the first glass of Sidi Brahim
you lay face to face touching each heart's braille, your necks on the vellum of leaves
swept up the ridge by last Sunday's flood, now you see
the air within the air.
You hear it because you believe it. There is no other sound.
Except this prelude to the breeze, its intrinsic forgetfulness.
Air will never be translated, it is within me to die with me.
I hear no rival sound but this in the landscape, the passage
that evolved with the conduit and the shattered clay pipes
at La Fourche where the air swore at the House of the Seven Children
I heard this rise, the air within the air, where you walked after breakfast
'to digest but picking every guava' along the banya road.
There is no notion of time until the wind blows,
there is no sense of time until the wind blows
no train of thought until the notion goes.

Heat beat the leaves at the tip of the columnar to paste,
strange insects swim the white air that circles your lovely waist
                        A country
                                formed of stars
to the Megellanic clouds
        you walk in air and not on the bone roads.
Sunlight cast this prayer through the long drapes
of water : welts where roches jutted up from green sagailles
of the river bright at the entrance to the eel cavern where
nickel, silver, a pannier sacré lay cached in oil skin
        breathing under the flutes of the tree racines
Roches are mournful mouths walked on by steers barging thru'
hedges of guava, in the grass light of March this side

the other side of the river, hurling green shadows on our waists and faces
    from hives of sunlight

In the grey ocean the tide breaks against what's between a crescent
and a lariat of beach near mangroves – there the water is pimiento –
and chases shoes that saw no laces, water that saw no current in mangroves
stagnant like slack despotisms where lianas grow strangling in water the tall
                                                                                  grass stalks arc
off the horizon's sand where there is sunlight and a long sickle of water

Air on the pliant saplings,
murals of rodeos under the spray paint
in the colonial houses, **F . L . N . K . S .**; Eloi Maturo the white
shells of theft pinned to the beams where air falls and swims like a music.
Assassiné. Ribbons of light where glass sliding doors shattered
where windshields shattered. Air breathing on the archipalego's carcass,
of blossoms and reflections, their pursuit of nickel
rays of air in water

A couplet of beechleaves in your hair;
beeswing swing, your cherrywood temples of
high spring silence,
two eyes of a freshly open oyster shell
carrying mother's enceinte green
east in the pupil

into scents pathing chosen glades
you grinned, you lit your path with thought
how often come home to Bourail a pleasure of greeting

but pardon my asking :
       you never defined your prize
for giving speech to the story
       of our first two summer years.

A day of moments we kissed, flattened
grass shoots, and Good Friday
walked into that countryside the very last time.

Insects swim the white air that circles your waist

Did you, did you plant your year
in slender beech – harbouring opal sun glint?

It is said we looked in this country for water hyacinths
but the south pole now separates us from them :
near velvet of columnar pines, half eaten guavas
destined to swell in the womb
you left – the garden lit with lemon trees

Going out to walk and digest,
but picking every guava

A passover seen as a farewell
denies us return, is, no more than
a blessed interlude

Needle and threadlessly columnars tower
over the path; dazed by the drugged interlude
we wake a cold stream with our laughter :
how close we are to departure, being sure that
heroes do make it both ways

Spelt

What are these fears that emote themselves in the canvassing of a hiccup when people of Melanesean blood cross marble floors in Nouméa? What does the phrase mean the gestural declension of blood is it to do with filleting of fish or what is the blood that comes to your cheek when you are running up the stairs and another is approaching how dare you shortchange me I demand at the very least to show impatience

I am quitting this island, I am quitting this continent with all I have appropriated in two in half, I think I will go through vide will go through the Declarations what have I to declare I am richly a neutral I am neither French, Caldoche nor Melanesean, what am I taking back to the public when I find them I'll show them what's what and what there is to be eager upon

In this vein of connecting I have spent a lot of time with my cheeks refreshed by the sun and I am coming back to Europe with my cerveau full of the regal names of fruits and birds and hunting implements and flowers that you will never know what I am taking about which means you will impeach me in some lubricating way or other

Now that it is time for me to pack my valise of night and that the renettes the chiens bleus the other fabrications are not disturbing me now I can look back on this island and say I have not invaded a paradise where I learned a thing or two but not recalled how I could learn because I am uncoordinated and what is there but southern comfort from the peachjuice of the sky

Ah yes you remember my comfort you remember my cheek you remember my straying behind in the *case* while everybody went out looking for pommes canelles or checking the nasse to find the holiest most priestly lobster that there was was there more to say I stood under the cradle shade up there in the sky and I saw the pencement that battleship grey halfring in sky where the moon had been and raising my throat up to the post where my elbow was tendrilled and even and fair in any game of knuckles or leave-down-over I recalled I had copulated so often on this island and now I knew that I had learned something but you appropriated the abricot coloured paper shiny on one side in the bottom of the camping [trunk] my mouth was higher than yours last Sunday night that was GORGEOUS and this was another which you could shine against it would not hurt you gosh grace nothing would grab me I was far from my premonitions and presentiments Which body did I see run through with a thick knife before the weekend, and whose body was undreamt of below cherryblossom?

In the parc closed at one gate way where two men and a woman caressed each other a plastic caravan stood lit by what was encased by battery and generator and there was no watching sport or spring hooked up to their caravan it was more of A CONSTRUCT THAT SHOULD NOT HAVE BEEN THERE AT ALL and while I was walking through Nouméa I discovered censorship did not extend to Gaston Gallimard and those whom his offspring published and stood there perusing Ernst Juenger Destouches *Le Livre Blanc* with the matelots' dicks spurting roman candles I especially liked that two handed book Marguerite Yourcenar's Fleuve negro spirituels Robert Desnos Max Jacob Guilliame Apollinaire when I read Ap I realised browsing was preferable to perusing and meant robbing but I was not in a mood for shoplifting I had other situations to get to grips with and that way the sun gave way to appearing for a little longer and I went to the Musée Canaque I knew that there were only weeks at most until people would endorse vigil-antes and there would be lynchings animosities and throat holes for the police but I did not envisage such a rhetorical blockbusting deliverance such as the G.I.G.N. taking out the hostages and executing them napalm

The woman's hair in the caravan oh yes we are back to that old storey that former novel if you like it I can arrange for you to have the author come to your terrasse and play you at noughts and crosses just to get things underway

The woman's hair was crowblack and heaped at almost the perimeter of her breasts, her back was small and covered although you could see sporadically her spine was teak

One dying and three living a liverish quality had you been consuming quantities of silver foil butter shipped in from Normandy "where were you father on Saint Crispin's Day?" "down the pub" it would heartburn you frying on wooden planks this liverish qualité took possession of blue green fields and allotments decayed plants and small parrots haphazard birds you know what is meant by keeping a stare on[1] and affiliated the reflections to those that are ricochet proof this caravan has a clammy-to-the-touch présentément but a hectare or two of decompouse will do no good in the long term but for the short edit it is a viable form of blotting paper

Sun lit down on all pollutants of the river they do not require inventories you can guess chutes pipettes and seepage

Your silhouette obroamatic gesturing with your lungs sieving full of air on a Silesian causeway just down the steps jut to the left thassright sssh I am out snaring in the tribu this is the this is just the endeavour an endorsed method of Assembling informatique – dont overlook that when you've demobbed my scathing particular One I do see foam around the head and lips purple bruises on the sternum pass me your stethoscope I am a beginner I gaze through that tube oh it is so big is that a borehole a hole for your vantage they'll do luxuriantly fine as the barometer goes up bashful your silhouette reaffirms and tumultuous cliffs of FLUORESECENT AEROSPACE hanger-pleasure the colony polling booths must surely disseminate from in the glands oh this much is true you distress-call me with your lymphing arm broken in that position ist possible to fracture 'in so many places' don't be coy describing me your pleasures – I say it is richly pleasing to inhale vapours than just drink and swallow you shall soon be airlifted out of here it is not human form but hyæna and Alsatian who shoal at helicopter launch pads not who but 'that' snarl because BEASTS do not have the equivalent possessive I can assure you that my mouth has been forced open be installed and gulping about that

1. *'Showing a stare'*

An Alpabetized Note on the Text

Acajou is a reddish wood, a false mahogany, sometimes called tar tree, with black sap, and can provoke lesions and swellings. There are 12 species of *arucaria* (*pin colonnaire*) they grow into vast columns, as much as 50 metres high. They are used for building *cases**. Bec-de-can is a coarse and pungent fish, popular with green bottle flies. *Canaque*, meaning 'men' is the name navigators gave to the original Melanesean inhabitants, *Kanak* is the contemporary, politicized spelling. A **case* is a traditional Melanesean dwelling, usually circular with mud walls and a tall, thatched roof. A *daoua* is a large white sea fish. The *flèche faitière* has been incorporated into the FLNKS flag, and is the ornamental wooden spear surmounting the roof of the grande case and symbolizing the unity of the clan. *Inyam* is a root vegetable. The *lunette* is a minute green bird with white spectacle rings round the eyes. The *métis* are people who are a recent mixture of French, with Melanesean, Javanese and or Vietnamese blood. *Monnaie Kanak* is a symbolic, social and economic object, a repository of 'coutum', of yesterday, today and tomorrow. Also known as *thewe*, made from the bones of fruit bats, shells and stones, all on a minutely sculpted string. The *thewe* (*monnaie Kanak*) is then wrapped in the skin of a fruit bat, to express support in social exchange. The *niaoulis* is a slender white tree with a pink shine in certain lights, resistant to bush fire. *Number One* is a local lager, which is delicious. *Panier sacré* – each family group possesses a "*panier sacré*", a money which is their heritage. It is always attached to an art object, finely crafted from mother-of-pearl. It is a sacred possession packed in a little pirogue, set in a neat net then wrapped in fireproof bark and leaves as protection against misfortune. A *petroglyph* is an ancient stone or rock on which symbols and images, patterns and shapes were carved in relief, symbolising cultural images of the *tribu** which created them. A *sagaille* is a spear that fish like *bec de canne* are caught with. *Taro* is a root vegetable. *Tribu* a tribe. The *tricot rayé* is a sea snake.

M. C.

Tandis que virent à Djibouti, dans la lune et les cris, les goudrons énormes des courriers du jeudi pour Mombaze, Zanzibar, Mayotte, Mazunga, Nossihé, Tamatave, La Réunion, Maurice ou, à Dakar, dans le soleil et les heurts sourds des barcasses, ceux du mercredi matin pour Konakry, Grand Bassam, Petit Popo, Grand Popo, Libreville.

Blaise Cendras, *Moravagine*

Once the hail had lifted,
pith hills with untraversable vantage points
you could see derricks and the single track railway, mebbe a shop front,
hills go down to cliffs   you come thru fields over a III-century mosaic,
you are now on river that opens into sea
it is before going to nightclub
you may walk with three pals loosely in their co.
   ach if you're insecure in their wake
but sand's layered and weltered
it is only   imprecise distance
to actual water; plateau alloy
embossed veneer
and
ya shoulda seen stars and glitter over the firth
but in my knees under the skin, stars skime
so cold and nonplus moan it makes me want to greet

   *A cold silvery mist had veiled the afternoon, and the moon was not yet
   up to scatter it.* (Charles Dickens)

FELDER LANDSCHAFT

A wash of fields
at dawn
— peony, Vertical
slitherer's teeth (The)
working your tongue round artificial cream
in the split doughnut
got at auctioneers' café. Go away Mr Whippy.
I do not hear anything but crickets
therefore often silence
I do not relate to anything

a sun rises over the fields

There is a spectral rising
like indigo wake I think
going up to the loch resistance to s-sacrifice

Registered
  this aura, silver threads
strafing from behind the eyes *threading* like non ending silver *neck* chain

Aura (nt)
it is colour and not colour
Absolutely, and patently not. *What do you say?*
                               What do you know?
                                           (James Cagney)

Come from Inverness, there is no city like it.
O Travel from the capital
to the coast. And then the sand walk.
Eventually the sea. Green grey headland froth

Because of the alcohol bruling refractory fracturing sloth
that furs in the divers neural foyers
Sheer
I am unable
to be precise other than it is a real lot of water
sloshing
       I can't just sit on a shooting stick pretend
       this never happened

'In one game, the players heads are smeared with treacle in a darkened room and a glowing preying mantis is released. Whoever the insect lands on, wins. In another, the competitors must run through a forest blindfolded with their hand behinds their backs. The winner is the last one to hit a tree.'

wide sloshing vagues gan to turquoise and green

metallic cable
grail

I miss my mother

The corn holds holidays that the sun doesn't know about
                                         (Tristan Tzara)

this cat engenders septicæmia
   in the pale wicker bird in
  one-pelt
(I go with marbles, row and roister)
    Let's go back
to the coast. Gulls
      bought their mocha of brine with them
        up in to the high street
  Over TV aerials That pelt pellmell
 billiard-table surface.

Why do the layers need
    replenishing?
I think I can pause on a note of
   beauty is difficult Yeats by Pound and all of that
élitist partisan angst   but I can't leave
without the waterskis
without the hydrofoil
 I think I can pause on a note of
variance endeavouring to register
the accords
Silent sluicing thru' the silver water
     bowsprit taking me (M.C.) out

It has been /
a long time, in steady cam
 points of vue Since she worked
and come past here   even
   past the back grilles the eternallyellowedcardboard
crates and detritus   shells McCains / findus / stovies /
what a pungent parquet flooring

      You can't just cross a road to write

I think I'd best not
  say a word, just nod
agree, get them deflected
  if they'd *only listen*

Straw slips into the edge
water, its tubes open out white

like mould, goose mud
    Some of this straw's blue like menthol TicTacs
so much it makes me [have to] greet
just like skies' slipped in the (straw) poles

'I wish he didn't get up out of bed so early'

On the banks, those lonely shores
fire-spilt past The Reservoir
    where they (at least three) ducked
after work and tried a round with me
(I nearly softened)

Cannibalism, Tago Mago, Return of The Upsetter, soundtracks. Ennio,
Jacques Brel, lee Hazlewood, Gerard Grisey,
    the sheets of paper are so blue
Rachmaninov, Blue Orchids, WIRE,   the carbonna trance
Kathleen Ferrier, Martin Carthy, prince Jimmy Scott
    tracing a liner which just swerved
Quatre Chants, Falling in love is Beautiful, FINE POWDER THIS HEAT
Disney Boys, Le Plat Pays some Velvet morning on the lonely shores
when I'm straight   the pebbledash banks

I'm going to open up
    your gate / and tell you about Phèdre
and how she let it slide   with your backpack
intransigence and awful uncool dumb bespeak
orange aisles where

orange aisles (how) he held his head so tight lunchtimes
and after midnight trying to hold all the
information IN Ronnie
Lane's   bringing both hands up
to the cheeks, trying to smile thru
the interlinked lights
slim chance

    This didn't coordinate

Bulb traps in moist post-sun grass splays. Moths
dangle on screen up on the hill, going in to the
crevasse, after a night under the bulb you are packaged into
the fridge.

I will walk with you in my company
I would press hands on the loins of the sea
Almighty undaunted oceans of South and
I would lie unto my harbour head and mend the boats

Yet this is not near, the sentiment cliff
nor my nightwatch which preserves the tawny of cereal
Escarp meant the one meal we shared
Before we were displaced
you to one permutation, I to another

*Life is empty and meaningless. It is in emptiness that we create
the possibility for extraordinary results.* (Aron Ralston)

PRE TROPICANS

In the simp
lest horizons facing orange
I can feel the sap rise the loins de lymph
& pother forms of hysteria
         Quick (if you are)
you can distance from *all-the-ominous*
  and retrench yourself in another piece of
This Globe

There is not a letter here for you

No reasonable sense of communication

         has prepared me for this
in my pale striped thin shouldered dress
  an orange doctor Martens
I am walking without looking a' left ta right

Granulated
  sugar
 bay. Precise and pre requisite

     Infantile and inertia
      I wish I
      hadn't got here

S.Y.L.P.H.

    Plenitudes the raucous hides
germinate what is otherwise Dis
    carded, Out & about weaving these pelts
drinking McEwans *until you curdle.*
  Dance. Step. Shoesole scraping on the pier

no sea
no spray
no san reno shops
no slo mo
(fun) hurtle
   despoil
[a]tion rummage
   thru' the hand
     bag find stripes phone and
glorious bag of rambles

TROPICANS

With my blue haiyre
which has gone grey due to paint
I have opened these nostrils wide
to have a stab at hearing
when can I get out to be barbaric
if it's suitable to grind
down to ammonite
certitude

I have left that shore
with a grey duffel bag slung
spinning over my sinew shoulders
I'll get to hitch some rides
and other times I'll ramble
ya must have seen these pano
   ramas when you were here   last

                        hop a train / stay and gamble
                        her
                        name's Codeine prettiest girl

                              you ever seen
Several counties down
         and not very fleeced
I have been bleeding (a little)
but mainly stock piling
residues for late CONSID
ERMENT
What I last said was certainly
that I fancied my driving instructor
but not more than that

Even though I keep swinging left
I know there are cliffs shores gorges east
and that perplexes me
as if I didn't feel   (presume I was going down
on one stocky transit at all, but simply
holding back as if I was still a kid in
the playground in a red hood coat holding skipping rope which
only hurt the back
of my handsknuckles

Seeping thru
         stems and lapels of
a prejudged coat
             where I am sitting hours
again on coastline
                 causing no effect
    other than
                     To rethink it all   To sit and dumb
                  ly go down
to basics and not know
         what I need
other than tea
One canny   Walk
man   Cluster /Eric
Satie towards the dark end
of the
         CUT
Street

Caution. Caution. I have not

    revealed anything layered over my tongue
        my flesh is pocked with blue
            I have moved with the transit
                and the champs are blue

I buttress in where I am gang
    echo and pitch   surface unsure
   I lie about I have sleep at odd hours
       the soft gym like matt I roll up
           take about   The one party I went
at was pathe
tic, she was naked
except an orange thong vomit on her
shoulder and in her hair a lot on the wall
opposite the bath tub
    where she was in the recovery
        position; the water gone the blue lights
           coming

Trees are blue and white and the road is
blue. A decrepit stone mason walks here with a cane
and fifteen sheep.

I will kill them all.

Unfurled, this roll of light,
dragging from the train
clanking in the opposite direction
of the imbecile with the flock. Heading backwards
or forwards with a small revolutionary knife
in my teeth, over my tongue I can roll
I can go and go spurting
cutting arteries and windpipes,
any useful conduit for blood and the nervous
  system I will undoe it

 A man with a cloth is unfurling paraffin
cases, paraffin canisters, paraffin spirit levels,
paraffin cement. I cannot dispense him
if I need, I want, I desire His
assistance in my creating a

morass with the sheep and their instructor.

Why I'm app
prehensive if I app
reciate what you
done – or did for me in getting me
out of that fix, and making me believe
it was *all* worth it – I couldn't
      greet alone   I did have to stay
           out in the field with three months
               worth of hedge outcuts
                    burning in a palace (straw)
keeping us warm all
and fixed to sights

I like it when
   sea's got oil eggs on it
in the moon's cool surface   turns it silver
white
green
blue Something shines   I'd like to
   gett there before any others, enjoy hanging
     in a rocking chair leaning back armstossed over back
       bantering nattering
Eventually I
   get dressed   smartish
    in a blue dress
nothing underneath / and wear
   size four Wellington
it'll be cold right   drink some port and wine
barly wine or Mackesons go out and jump a train
   lots of scope to go rambling

this etchy sketch
  plan I think it's
ten sketch Something shines I have a mouth of
       cortisone We watch W.Wing
         go out at 10 ish, much like moths along the sea street
its double cold

(SEE)
I SPY A DARK STRANGER

(Deborah Kerr)

I scat away from the gang, the sore head
burst wee chicks and when my fortunate foster
uncle hauled me on the train I ended up broke
yet a woke and [k]new enough for a job

But the hours of cleaning Bored me, and
  when the train arrived
Kings Cross was a land of PILFERERS

  Marginally and much later on
blemished, this coast you
  (you can have for keeps) sensate
    dimension look just look at guillemot

    swirling tide, come down
      to blister flesh, up the lippy
unsurpassed
    wine

slap it on
    G Hoon talking about Saddam
this announcement I
  make Saddam won't climb down, grinds on
like a budgerigar fucking a pig

The Verdict on Hunger

Fly doon like a corbie thru a shoal of shoes
 whose eye roams the bread
lake yeah croaks : Wait! V'Attend!
I come from telegraph wire

 This conduit of paper
ARCED LIKE BEAUTIFUL ARROWTIPS,
 it doesn't mean anything your driving lessons your life :
Discman!

Nice wan,
tapping like a leg

on a maribou stork
getting greety on the M62 register
 passing down Cumbria
  go out left just there
see the grey sloots of sky equidistant from the last roller
like s'got all up mixed with
dunes Dunes'
sky has
uh.
 Okay. There. The blue cills
  you know, the ones that you see
   in that tipe of climate climax
    within the dunegrass
     where
        you pare away the stems and

Go away Peedy Mary
get out of the alley
it's as not a blue steer I'm after
having, but a gem up
on driving lessons
a tautology if I ever
heard one
Go away Jealous Ghenghis
get out of the harbour car park
it's not a green day a ticket
for a trolleyrun in Harvey
Nicks when I get Edinbro'
–but an ultra loop
the Eternal if ever I
hear
Come near er CrowHEAd
maized wee kitten
with a shitray made outta a
1.5 kg Cornflakes box and a lotta topsoil
 Crow Ed Crow Ed
you're the one for me Crow Ed
 white and ginger
ly nimble flitting
 over the rooves to gett
here

early See
your the one for me   ah hm

window open

A SHORT ABOUT LOVE

I bring mail from the town
 and pass it round/thru yr door
I leave milk at your flat
and tho I've not learned to prey
I wait till evening and you come home
I want so much to love you more

   see you more

Now it is ten
time to get up shake it all
about
you'll not be staying long
do you have staying power?
how long have you the
  you can stay it off so long
and get granted a stay of
exhortion
 distinction
Something is not plain speech.
I know that. I have not been court
with a silver rucksack making
tea bitter as hops
 a periwinkle pickled herring vealhampie
        broadbeans big as a bulldog's bollocks
ah salver for the dinner I am having
        down in Aberwystwyth
Well. Near it.
Two chapples, oh so very tall
and thin walled –
Your dapper, beautiful
  beauteous floorboards
all the windows broke, the leads

   nicked. One was ment
  to be converted
 a while ago. A few years.
  Both the money ran out

Something is not plain speech
& never was. You can't subscribe
to the unusually cavalier pos
ition of making ends meet
without contributing something   I know I would fynde
   it hard in my haart to stop you enjoying
       your newfound snog with your newfound beau
        in your newfound cruiser as you goe
         thru' all the positions of
  reversing and three point [3.] turning
  with the instructor ignoring me as if I'd never
payed my own lessons as I stood there yearning
dumbass stupid marking you Hanna
get in for a lesson the first one is Half Price
this is not this is not
the system so I'm just hoiking
up my rucksack and sleepover bag
with four hundred pounds liquid
in my seersucker pocket
 going off on one myself (that means own steam see)

Looking at Samantha Morton on the large
 screen, well ish the wan cinema
 on the Back Settlement, S.M. who doesn't say
  anything being mute or deaf or something I don't know
   I am blasted I like violent sex and am
    on the lookout for it if it comes
's well and good   doanrightdisgusting but I dont sustain it
I shiver greet a lot and can't decipher
So go out with a reverse button pressed
to turn over cassette to find BeBopDeluxe
crying to the skies, schwon schwahn   crying / to-the /
skies, sczhwarn sczhwarn I have cleered my throattuh / tettuh / tuttuh uh uh
    sssstetetetahtetuttee I have a little (pron. lettle) surprise
angels *don't goad me*
crying to the skies. I made IT in heaven

cautious lidless eyes on
shoulder / you have to watch
for cues / my expression banks no
repute / I have to hold you
tonight tehtashtetut uh uh huh huh, sailing our bodies (like stalks
on seeds) up over / the Ooohhh/cean
without lov
   we are all spent
without lov
  we are all gone
without love / holding us togggether / we are not human / we are ships in
the night
going our own way going our own way
going our own way together out to the
ocean, looking back together sailing
out however,
Ships in the Night

Crying-out at Chap
El Perilous putting my white hands
together keeping the phinal
 night-without a warning
as a harried vigil
sssstaying my powers off
sssucumbing to his embraces slips
placing his rowdy salty lips round me
 keeping me on the unsheeted out
of the bed as I'm looking
forward to the vulgar window
look out cold silver stars condensed milk powder smell

 to the sky

crying to the sky

Walking out of a vegetable silence

 because she was reely stupid
 really across the shore
with little sandflecks getting between my toes
hard like glass
mainly, cos so cold
     with evergreens hanging off cliffs

                    I don't even know why I am pulled to these edges
Means when I get there
I don't look far out at *the* distance

Prefer fires myself
stoking them up and letting them
blaze then ebb down a white hot
skislope for little snappy twigs
AND BREATHE IN THE SCENTS AND CARRY THE BITS
    IN MY THROAT FOR TWO DAYS AFTER

        AND SMELL OF SMOKE AND YOU CAN'T LIGHT
        A FIRE ON THE SEA CAN YOU?

So-breaking out of the sea
canyon
I refil my brand new dancing bag
            The Rucksack
three pairs sunglasses
one t shirt red with a logo
tight
four cassettes one C120
a pair of sexy on the hips and ass
thin cordorouys with metal studs (maroon)
a address pad, camra
2 reel of films to dvlp
a bra if I go to a wine bar only
(pale claret)
lippy, Sleepy Deepy pills one book *er*
knut h Two really R.D.Laing *Knots*
the cassettes, home made!
Softinthehead – Billy Mackenzie
Joe Ely
Alex fucking Harvey, FRAMED, Small Axe
Kevin Coyne
augustus pablo patrik
fitzgerald   john
jacob niles ali farka
toure
ronnie 'plonk' lane *Weightless Again*

a quick one while he's away

well i'm out on the road, hitching
   in a van full of parts
Zanussi parts   think it's as Zanussi ach
just reeding with the vehicle cluster
    on the motor-
way, south of
south of something
 Devoid of something
Out they go, Blesséd and Contained
  remote from the threat fields
when little paths get invisible ghosts
     of yellow tape sudden spring up
Away from the fields the stoggs the trolls the erosions
the corbies the topsoils the sort of conversions
the left-out posters the bi-ways (don't mind bi ways)
all the stuff that makes for a green and pleasant land
I prefer
where I am, kind of sitting
room'd, with beakers and mag lites
and wire removers in a parts van

Cold mushrooms
something else
on the plate
 silver silos, in the cold cold cold
stackrooms in the deep deep silos
 where the world on its thumb turns
  in the sad sad trailers
     and the blown blown marriages
    and the cold cold summer lease floats in December
and the
gash
of blood when the countries go to war
knocking at the microdots with the
clusterbombs B.singing like a pilot
when the DAISI bombs
wreck
and roam

  or something
it was set in the D Depression, a love

    triangle lots of picking Django
        Reinhart's closest friend I can't remember
a pretty girl pretty enough for me

and out in the silencing sun to where
the batteries to the generator went sulphorous
    and could have blown me up
        where I last was eking out a (not a way of life but)
            manner of extisens
no bother. Out in the silencing sun that
hurts if everybody is in it and I am not
but a Picasso woman in a
seal hood that I am certain
with that boy being a real dildo
   not passing out on anything to say
      he made me clammy up my oxters
         and that never happen before
seeing the pit of my stomach
uncoil literal as I look
over my stomach under the
freath lights with my stomach
    swelling like I oughta cut

food out for three days and just sleep
coouried with my face near the window

        FIN

CONTENTS

HER GENTLE SLAB

Syd Barrett Refrigerator	9
Work Don't Worry	15
Abstraction du Temps	17
The Five Squibs	19
Scythes in the gorse bushes ...	22
Pantone 627	23
The Lighthouse and the Clam	25
Bye Bye Blackbird : Slight Return	28
Liaïson	30
Accidental Sightings	31
To the Spirit of Andrei Tarkovsky	36
Als the Sadwe in the Undermel	37
The Stars Have Broken in Pieces	40
Very slowly drawn ...	45
Borzage	46
The Heron	47
Sea Mortar	50
The Funeral of David Gascoyne	53
The Girl and the Dog	55
Sans Toit, Ni Loi	59
Poem	61
S.W.	62

LISTENING TO THE STONES

R.SV.P. Edward Thomas	73
The hour of escape	74
A Holiday	75
The Pathways of Guava	77
Summer in Dream	80
For Louis Tjibaou, Sculptor	82
Hienghène	85
Dawn	92
I Dreamed I Dream : Ouvea	93
Prayer	96
At night the sleeping rain …	97
The Difference between Sunlight and a Wedding in Pothée	98
The Air Is On Fire	100
A couplet of beechleaves in your hair	102
Spelt	103
AFTERWORD	106

M. C. 107